ONE STOP *Meetings*

The One Stop Series

Series editor: David Martin, FCIS, FIPD, FCB
              Buddenbrook Consultancy

A series of practical, user-friendly yet authoritative titles designed to provide a one stop guide to key topics in business administration.

Other books in the series to date include:

ONE STOP
Meetings

DAVID MARTIN

 ICSA Publishing

Published by ICSA Publishing Limited
16 Park Crescent
London W1N 4AH

© Buddenbrook Consultancy 2000

Typeset in 10/12.5 pt Meridien
by Fakenham Photosetting Ltd, Fakenham, Norfolk

Printed and bound in Great Britain by
T J International Ltd, Padstow, Cornwall

British Library Cataloguing in Publication Data

A catalogue record for this book is available from the British Library

ISBN: 1–86072–117–6

oral, written, spoken
verbal / non-verbal   *speaker*   *technological*

Contents

Preface

In every way in every day countless meetings take place – some formal – or not, some planned – or not, some purposeful – or not. Meetings are an integral part of our society in every aspect of its operation regardless of age, sex, colour, creed and political affiliation. An incredible number of decisions are taken (and many deferred) during these events.

Despite their importance in terms of decision-making, few of us receive any training to deal with such a fundamental part of the control of organisations. Even my professional training as a Fellow of the Chartered Institute of Secretaries concentrated on the legalities of meetings, resolutions and company law, but gave no coaching on the practicalities of preparation, negotiation and contribution which are such essential aspects of productive meeting work.

Indeed, very often we learn how to deal with meetings by being at them and seeing how others perform – both well and poorly – and of learning the hard way when our tactics did not work and others needed to be adopted. As the proportion of better educated and more aware citizens continues to grow, the discussion of issues in meetings (of all types) is likely to become tougher – and the challenge to get our views across more effectively could become more difficult. The days when, for example, employees were told to keep their heads down and get on with their work without asking questions are well and truly past. A greater proportion of employees are more likely to want to know a greater range of information concerning their employers and their prospects. Consultants McKinseys estimated that early in the twenty-first century, 70 per cent of all European jobs will require professional skills (that is A-level grade or higher) whilst the remaining 30 per cent will require skills that are only marginally less. The Confederation of British Industry commented that *'outstanding communication skills'* will be needed by these employees.

If meetings are to be productive and efficient, we need adequate skills for dealing with what this book seeks to provide help, that is, 'the meeting challenge'. However, it is not simply communication skills that are needed, but a degree of preparedness which experience indicates not all participants have. That is the aim of this book – to identify a number of instances when participants will be taking part in a meeting and then to place before the reader a number of aspects needing attention prior to use in those situations – and some tools to use to achieve our aims and the meeting's aims. Inevitably in dealing with some matters within a limit of 80,000 words, only an overview can be provided, but it is hoped that in each case sufficient has been included:

- to give an indication of the areas that need attention;
- to prompt questions and further thought; and
- to provide guidance regarding dangers and threats.

In the text I have quoted Harvard Professor J. K. Galbraith, who once said: 'Meetings are indispensable when you don't want to do anything.' There is no doubt that a number of 'meetings without meat' as we describe them here, do take place every day up and down the country. Perhaps, human nature being the way it is, this situation will never be eradicated, nevertheless, given the amount of time the average manager spends in meetings (as much as 40 per cent of the week) we should try:

- to identify a purpose;
- to prepare and make ourselves more effective before, during and after the meeting;

in order:
- to make our meetings more effective.

Included within the essentially practically oriented content are a number of references to the need to take what some may regard as somewhat devious methods to achieve one's ends. Obviously, such devices should only be used when the alternative seems to be the fulfilling of Professor Galbraith's aphorism. Very often, meetings and meeting members will be productive – and these aspects of this book may be unnecessary. However, in other situations, such sections (easily located using the expanded index format of the *One Stop* series) may be of assistance.

Happy (and productive) meetings!

David M. Martin
Buddenbrook, April 2000

Note:

The masculine has been used for simplicity's sake only. Other than in case studies, wherever the masculine is referred to it should be taken to include the feminine.

Meetings

Introduction: setting the agenda

Introduction

'Meetings take minutes and waste hours.' 'Meetings are indispensable when you don't want to do anything.' If either this old saying or the quote from Professor Galbraith holds good for meetings in which you or your organisation are involved, remedial action is needed. Such action may be as simple as ensuring that each meeting's aims are clarified and promulgated and that all participants are constantly reminded of and brought back to the task of attaining such aims. However, that accepts the inevitability of the need to hold the meeting in the first place and there is no doubt that many 'wasted hours' are spent in meetings which need never have been held. Before framing an agenda that will guide us like a map through what some commentators call the 'maze of a meeting', we need first to consider our 'agenda' in holding a meeting in the first place – and decide the kind of meeting it is to be.

What is a meeting?

A 'meeting' is dictionary-defined as 'an encounter or public gathering of people for a purpose', or 'an assembly of people for discussion'. If these are the best definitions of meetings, at least in business terms, and are used as guides by convenors and participants, then it is hardly surprising that so many meetings are ineffective. In attempting to provide a framework within which we can ensure we get the most from meetings, surely we need a more closely focused definition. This may utilise extracts from both the above, but must incorporate some essential ingredients that neither

Meeting – a new definition

A gathering of essential participants (only), each of whom has something to contribute, to discuss a problem touching on all their interests, to arrive at certain decisions, all as required by the predetermined aim(s) of the meeting itself.

— they waste so much time.

1

these two definitions addresses – the need for a meeting to have both purpose and aim and the need for meetings to take decisions.

This is obviously a far lengthier definition than perhaps space allows in
most dictionaries but does, by including elements of control dynamism and
purpose, set parameters by which we can work towards convening an effective meeting.

Do we really need a meeting?

Some people apparently live by meetings. Equally, some organisations
seem unable to operate except by meetings. Whilst many must be productive it seems reasonable to challenge why there is such a propensity for
holding so many meetings. Often the answer is that 'we've always done it
that way' – which may be true, but is hardly a convincing response. When
considering convening a meeting (which can be seen to be costly if one
calculates the cost per working minute of all those present) perhaps the
first question should be 'do we really need to meet?' In other words:

- before agreeing to hold a meeting we should challenge its existence
  (this is even more true of regular meetings than one-offs); and
- before discovering how to use the process of meeting to serve a purpose, we should consider alternative, and possibly more cost-effective,
  ways of achieving the same end.

> **Note**
>
> Research indicates that people reach better decisions when they occupy
> adjacent physical space than when they are remote from one another.
> This is a telling argument in favour of holding a meeting rather than
> trying to reach a decision by telephone, e-mail or the like, however it
> does not negate the argument that the *reason* for the meeting should
> be determined.

Since experience shows that a large number of purposeless or MEATLESS
MEETINGS are held, one objective of the challenging of existence of all
meetings should be to ensure that each does have sufficient 'meat', and
indeed 'meat of the correct flavour', to warrant convening or continuation.
Unfortunately meetings are often held:

a) that lack any real purpose, simply because it is a matter of habit;
b) for the wrong reason(s), which will automatically generate the wrong
   decisions;
c) as a method of shifting responsibility from an individual to a collective
   basis;

> **Note**
>
> Since there is a widespread tendency to promote above the level of competence – the Peter Principle – which results in some people operating at a level above that for which their talents and experience suit them, this may encourage the overpromoted to protect their positions by seeking a meeting to take responsibility for decisions which are properly their own.

d) as a delaying or spoiling tactic. If a swift decision is essential for the success of the project, deferral to a meeting may either kill it off, or ensure that its success is marred or rendered impossible. In meeting-oriented organisations, decision delays can occur because they are not taken until everyone can fit a meeting into their schedules, which may be congested simply because of the sheer number of other meetings! In addition, because decisions are usually taken in meetings or after discussion in meetings, decision-makers or managers may become timid, afraid to take decisions on their own account; or

e) as a means of achieving a 'hidden agenda', that is moving towards a decision which has an effect additional to those visible and recognised by most people.

Types of meetings

Assuming a meeting is to be held and has sufficient 'meat', its type must be determined. There are a variety of meetings and attempting to reach a conclusion using the wrong type may be as counter-productive as a holding a meeting 'because we always have'.

Face to face

This involves two parties coming together either by mutual design at a preset time, or by deliberate design of one of them waylaying the other, or by an entirely unplanned encounter. In the first two instances at least one of the parties will have had an opportunity to prepare for the meeting, which is essential if the encounter is to be effective. The party waylaid by deliberate design and both parties meeting by accident will have had no chance to research the matters for discussion or to prepare their views or case(s). With such a background an acceptable outcome may be unlikely.

Impromptu informal gathering

This is usually set in action by, say, a senior person suggesting that a few interested parties 'get together and thrash out a solution'. The problem for most members again is that they will be caught unawares, with little time to consider the subject matter whilst the urgency and enthusiasm of the instigator may be difficult to resist, particularly if (s)he is their senior. Because the meeting is convened in a rush its purpose may be unfocused and unclear. There is thus a danger of its taking far more time than is necessary, since the questions and arguments of each participant will be enunciated in an unstructured way reflecting their lack of preparation. This can be compounded if the instigator is someone who acts on instinct and has set up the meeting with insufficient thought and planning. In this instance the arguments and pressure of the instigator may themselves take time to crystallise, the discussion thus becoming circular rather than progressive. In being diverted from other work, the participants' effectiveness may be considerably impaired. Although difficult to resist, if previous occurrences demonstrate that such meetings tend to be less than effective, participants may need to:

a) discover the subject matter swiftly; and
b) attempt to delay the 'immediacy' of the gathering to allow some thinking time.

BRAINSTORMING

This is a development of the impromptu informal and can be very effective particularly where the aim is the development of creative ideas which by their very nature are innovative and which, in order to 'flow' require interaction with, as well as reaction from, others (see separate section).

Ad hoc committee

This has similarities to the 'impromptu informal' although will normally be more structured to the extent of having an agenda and probably a pre-set time. The concept allows time for advance thought. Such meetings tend to be informal and can often be very productive. The purpose of such a committee is usually to consider specific business and following its conclusion the meeting members are disbanded. That being so, those appointed should be given not only detailed terms of reference, but also a date by which their conclusions and recommendations should be reported. If these controls are not installed, the deliberations of the committee can be unnecessarily extended by its members. Whilst normally only those really qualified to consider the subject matter should be appointed (not least since supernumeraries can have the effect of blunting the effectiveness of the others), the inclusion of a few members from entirely different backgrounds can stimulate the meeting discussions.

Regular committee

This description covers a wide range of meetings often given other titles, for example, executive, board, and so on. These tend to create a formality of their own and to be planned some time in advance. They may also be described as standing committees, that is they have a continuing role as opposed to the ad hoc, single-subject role. As such these meetings tend to consider routine business for the most part but with ad hoc business which may be of quite a wide-ranging nature, included irregularly. The widespread use of such meetings should not generate complacency regarding its effectiveness. Like every other meeting, it needs controlling in order to be effective, although the fact that regular business is required to be considered may exert a control of its own. A strong Chairman is required in order to ensure the ends or aims of the meeting are achieved within a reasonable time-frame. In part this may be achieved by referring suitable business to sub-committees which are required to 'report back'. The main meeting need then only consider business on an 'exception basis'.

Formal

These meetings tend to deal mainly with routine matters and may provide final authority for decisions possibly hammered out at a meeting with subordinate authority. Whilst there are some overtones of the 'rubber stamp' type of body, this can be dramatically changed if controversial matters need decisions. Very often such meetings retain only vestiges of decision recommending even though they may be the ultimate policy control authority.

External meetings

Most of the meetings referred to in this book are internal, with all members working for the same organisation. Although internal politics will play a role, this can be controlled by the Chairman and even countered by members themselves. This becomes more difficult in the external meeting where members attend as representatives of various organisations. Although the meeting itself may well have a clear purpose, this may not be in accordance with the wishes of any of its individual members – some of whom may be working to a 'hidden agenda'. Nevertheless some kind of consensus will be sought. In preparing for this kind of meeting members need to:

a) discover the aim of the meeting;
b) discover the attitude and preference of their own organisation. This may have to be presented on a 'sliding scale', running from the ideal preference, through acceptable compromises to an unacceptable position (see NEGOTIATION). In such a meeting situation some degree of

compromise is almost inevitably to be required and it will be impossible
to satisfy the preferences of all involved;

c) discover as much as possible about the other member organisations and
their representatives in order to assess their likely preferred and fall-
back positions. This will require a certain amount of research, but such
preparation may be well rewarded if only at a personal level. After all
if, on meeting another delegate, a member is able to refer to that
person's background, it encourages respect and may start an 'alliance',
which can be used later. However in carrying out such research one
does need to ensure it is accurate.

Public meetings

Other than for public enquiries, this type of encounter hardly fits the
revised definition of the word 'meeting', since the normal purpose is for the
speaker to use the opportunity to deliver a point of view or information –
and not necessarily to generate reaction. Obviously the speaker will need
adequate preparation for such an encounter which will include trying to
outguess the audience so that awkward questions and criticism are established, and more importantly satisfactory answers are framed, in advance.
This may enable the force of the question to be dealt with before it is asked.
Drawing the sting of the unsympathetic delegates should help the speaker
attain the aims. Members of the audience wishing to question or criticise
the speaker rarely rehearse their comments or practise speaking. Valuable
points can be lost simply because the speaker does not know how to put the
point across cogently or clearly. Obviously this works to the advantage of
the main speaker, although normally such comments should be treated
with respect no matter how badly they are presented. Ridiculing a speaker
with communication problems may well backfire on the main speaker, particularly with UK audiences, who tend to have inherent sympathy with the
underdog. Inadequate expertise at presenting arguments and using tactics
can lose the game, regardless of the value of the argument – guidance
which applies to all meetings of course.

PRESENTATIONS

In this format the participants tend to resemble the teacher–pupil relationship rather than delegates with more or less equal stature. The format needs
careful handling by the presenter to avoid disruptive elements wasting delegates' time and is dealt with in a separate section.

Agenda

Introduction

A meeting has been described as a maze with the Agenda as its map. Ideally, a meeting should never be as complicated as a maze, but nevertheless an Agenda can still serve as the map to guide the members, and particularly the Chairman, through the items for discussion. Despite having this potentially valuable role, often an Agenda is given scant attention and exists simply as a list of the various items of business to be considered at the meeting. This misses an opportunity not only to provide a guide to the members of the meeting, but also to identify what is required to come out of the meeting, that is, framing proposed resolutions and decisions. Without attempting to present the members with a *fait accompli* this can assist focusing the minds of those present on the point of the meeting. Within the Agenda it may also be possible to remind members of the aims of the meeting itself, that is, its purpose.

Finally, unless meetings are convened properly by means of a notice containing an agenda, decisions taken may be invalid.

Aims of the meeting

Meetings should have aims to try to avoid what can otherwise become an aimless discussion. Very often the inclusion of business on an agenda provides implicit rather than explicit short-term aims, which are not written down other than possibly within a budget or plan document. Conversely, longer-term aims may be set down in writing in a strategic document – although then not necessarily referred to during the meeting. The fact that such aims exist is to some extent, in convening a routine meeting, taken for granted although it may be advisable from time to time to set out such aims simply to act as a means of focusing the attention of the members on the criteria adopted.

Thus a Board of Directors might adopt for its regular meetings, aims such as follow:

a) maximise profit to at least £X million in the current financial year without utilising additional capital;

b) keep employment costs to not more than 25 per cent of gross margin;
c) earn Y per cent return on capital employed;
d) achieve output of 105 per cent of previous financial period;
e) maintain quality and service, to levels as defined;
and so on.

These are outline statistical guidelines or strategies, within which it is possible to adopt a number of alternative actions or tactics. Since the horizon and timetable of action of the Board are essentially long-term, providing the meeting achieves its overall aims, short-term deviations may be acceptable. It may be necessary to remind members of the aims to help keep the priorities focused.

Sourcing agenda items

Inevitably the construction of an Agenda will depend very much on the type of meeting required – but equally the efficiency of the meeting can depend how constructively the Agenda is compiled. If it is a regular monitoring meeting, it could comprise items drawn from the following sources.

Checklist

1. an annual list of items to be considered at set times (e.g. the dividend, preliminary announcement);
2. items to be considered or reconsidered requested from the previous or earlier meetings;
3. new business arising since the previous meeting out of the operation of the organisation;
4. items requested to be considered by members (individual house rules may apply to these items – e.g. they may be required to be approved by the Chairman prior to inclusion);
5. regular reports (accounts, cash forecast, contracts, etc.);
6. market, economic or legal changes affecting the business;
7. statutorily (or similarly) required items (e.g. approval of the report of the directors and annual accounts for submission to the AGM, dividend recommendation, etc.);
8. original material, possibly generated by the Chairman as a result of his responsibility for driving the meeting and the company forward.

Defining the results

Whilst with a routine meeting much of the business will consist of regular reports which, unless remedial action is required, will tend to be 'nodded through', inevitably there will be some items that will require decisions –

possibly on a one-off basis. It may be helpful to the members (as well as being a sound foundation for the preparation of the minutes of the meeting) to set out a draft of the decisions required (or even alternatives).

In the section on MINUTES is a suggested record for a regular meeting of the Board. The Agenda for that meeting utilising this concept might appear as follows:

ANY COMPANY LTD

AGENDA

for a meeting of the Board of Directors to be held on
8 March 2001
in the Board Room [at the registered office] at 10.00 a.m.
Board aims: [see example above]

Business:

1. Minutes of Board and Annual General Meetings held on 7 February 2001 (drafts attached)

2. Shareholder matters
[In accordance with the Board's request of [date] we have investigated the possibility of transferring the share registration work of the company and a REPORT is attached. The Board will be asked to approve that Share Registrars Ltd be appointed to act as the Company's registrars – see report attached.]

3. Finance
    i)   Management accounts to end February 2001 (attached)
    ii)   Depreciation
[It is proposed to charge depreciation at 33.3 per cent on a straightline basis on vehicles, office equipment and computers.]
    iii) Capital expenditure (see Capex form Numbers ... attached)
    iv)   Cash flow (statement to 30 June 2002 to be tabled)
    v)   Vehicle replacement
    vi)   Bank mandate
[The Bank has requested a new mandate a copy of which is attached. This differs from the existing mandate only in so far as (details)]
    vii) Overdraft
[We need to extend the overdraft by £100,000 and have applied to the Company Bankers for this facility, which is within the limits set in the Articles of Association.]

4. Current trading
[A report analysing the trading results over the five years to December

---

2000 of product X will be distributed by the Managing Director by 4 March]

5.   Personnel
[i. Report re proposals for trade union negotiations re wage review due 1 September is attached. Decision re action required.
ii. A report from the Secretary regarding current Health and Safety legislative requirements will be tabled.]

6.   Property
[The monthly report on property activity is attached. Decisions are required regarding items [detail] and further information regarding items [detail] will be available at the meeting.]

7.   Sealing

8.   Meeting timetable
[It is proposed to add 30 August, 27 September, 25 October, 29 November and 20 December to the list of Board meetings for the rest of the year.]

With an established Board, the Secretary might take the above a stage further and actually draft minutes for some of the uncontroversial matters and incorporate these in the Agenda.

One-off meetings

The same principle can be applied to one-off meetings as shown in the following example:

ANY COMPANY LIMITED

AGENDA

for an informal executive meeting to be held on
14 June 2001
in the Company Boardroom at 2 p.m. prompt
Subject: Absenteeism

Aims of meeting: To devise and implement up to five tactics or initiatives for immediate implementation to reduce absenteeism to near or below the industry average.

Items for discussion

1. To consider monthly reports of staff absenteeism over past 12 months (See résumé attached)

2. To compare such reports with analyses of absenteeism throughout the industry (See report from [Industry] Trade Association attached)

3. To consider whether there are special reasons for this company's poor performance, and if so what can be changed / improved to ensure a reduction

4. To determine five or more methods to ensure such a reduction.

Note: Members will be expected to attend with ideas (capable of implementation in the immediate future) for consideration.

Administration: The meeting duration will be two hours
                 No interruptions or messages
Attendance: Personnel Director, Company Nurse, Company Secretary, Works Manager, Sales Manager

Issued by (convener)   1 June 2001

Notes

1. setting the meeting over a week ahead should allow thinking time;
2. providing internal statistics with external comparisons sets the problem in context with time between Agenda delivery and holding the meeting allowing time for assimilation of the data;
3. requesting members' ideas ensures accountability;
4. stating that there must be no interruptions not only allows meeting members to brief their staff but also underlines the importance attached to the subject by the Chairman. It is not unknown for some meeting attenders to arrange for deliberate interruptions to meetings either to enable them to escape some agenda items or simply to try to bolster their own importance;
5. the tone and structure of the agenda itself seeks to demonstrate that action is required. It implies an urgency since the subject needs urgent rectification.

Shareholder meetings

1. Annual

Every public limited company (PLC) and, unless it has adopted an elective resolution *not* to hold Annual Meetings, every private limited company (LTD) must hold an Annual GENERAL MEETING (AGM) within 18 months of its date of incorporation and thereafter each calendar year and at intervals of no more than 15 months. To such AGM all those entitled to attend (that is, all shareholders) must be invited and be given adequate notice.

At such a meeting certain standard business can be transacted and the Articles should be checked for any special arrangements. If business other than that covered in the draft Agenda below is to be considered, then full details must be given as almost certainly such business will need a Special or Extraordinary resolution and the specific requirements of those resolutions must be complied with.

Whilst accidental failure to give notice to one or more member will not usually invalidate the meeting, every effort should be made to ensure that addresses are kept current and the Agenda/Notice is sent properly.

ANY COMPANY LIMITED

N O T I C E

is hereby given that the
Xth ANNUAL GENERAL MEETING
of the members of the company will be held at 9.30 a.m. at the [registered office] on Wednesday, 21 November 2001, for the purpose of considering the following business:

1. Notice of meeting
2. Apologies for absence
3. Directors' report for the year ended 30 June 2001
4. Profit and Loss a/c for the year ended 30 June 2001 and Balance Sheet as at that date
5. Retirement and proposed re-appointment as directors of
   a) Ms C. Smith
   b) Mr B. Jones
      who retire by rotation and, being eligible, offer themselves for re-appointment.
6. Retirement and proposed re-appointment as a director of Mr A. Robinson who was appointed a director on 1 January 2001, retires and offers himself for re-election.
7. Appointment and remuneration of auditors

By order of the Board

[Name]
Secretary   17 October 2001
A member entitled to attend and unable to do so may appoint a proxy to vote in his/her place. Such proxies should be sent to the Registered Office of the company to arrive not later than 48 hours before the commencement of the meeting.

Notes

1. Members must be given a specified number of days' notice of their meetings. Under existing Company Law 21 clear days (that is, ignoring the day of posting and day of the meeting) must be given for an AGM. However under the Stock Exchange listing agreement, PLCs are required to give their shareholders 20 clear business days' notice (thus intervening weekends and public holidays must be excluded).
2. If the Secretary is also a director, he/she should sign 'On behalf of the Board'.
3. Many Articles of Association require a proportion of the Directors to retire at each AGM and to offer themselves (if eligible) for re-election. Special Notice is required to appoint or re-appoint a director over age 70, and, for a public company an explanation of why it is appropriate that such a director to be appointed should be included (this is not a legal requirement but a requirement sought by bodies representing institutional shareholders).
4. Any director who has been appointed since the previous AGM must retire and can (if eligible) offer himself for re-election. The purpose being to ensure that the authority of the members is obtained for all Board appointments.
5. Special rules apply regarding the appointment at a general meeting of anyone other than the retiring Auditors.
6. Only members and auditors have a right of attendance at a General Meeting, although non-shareholding directors have a right of attendance should their dismissal or non-appointment be under consideration.

2. Extraordinary

Every General Meeting which is not an Annual Meeting is an Extraordinary General Meeting (EGM). EGMs are usually convened for specific purposes, although there is nothing to stop such business being conducted at the AGM provided adequate notice is given and the timing is appropriate.

ANY COMPANY LTD

NOTICE

is hereby given that an
EXTRAORDINARY GENERAL MEETING
of the members of the company will be held on Thursday, 13 December 2001 at 11 a.m. at [registered office of the company] for the purpose of considering the following business:

1. Notice
2. Apologies for absence
3. SPECIAL RESOLUTION: that the share capital of the company be and it hereby is increased from £10,000 to £2,000,000 by the creation of
   a) 990,000 new ordinary shares of £1 each ranking in all respects *pari passu* with the 10,000 existing ordinary shares of £1 of the company,
   b) the creation of 1,000,000 [X] per cent net p.a. Cumulative Redeemable Convertible Preference Shares of £1.
4. SPECIAL RESOLUTION: that the name of the company be changed to ANY OTHER COMPANY LTD

By order of the Board

[Name]
Secretary   10 November 2001

Notes

1. 21 days' notice are required of Special Resolutions so that even though an EGM only requires 14 days' notice the longer notice must be given.
2. Special Resolutions require a majority of 75 per cent of those present and voting.
3. Special Resolutions must be filed with the Registrar of Companies within 14 days of being passed.

Timetable

With Board and other formal meetings, certain business needs to be transacted at set times of the year and the timing of these requirements should be reflected in the list of meeting dates which should be prepared for at least a year ahead. This could include firm dates for (say) nine months, with suggested dates for later meetings which would be confirmed by an updated timetable issued on (say) a rolling six-month basis. This list should incorporate reference to such business, e.g. dividend payment, preliminary announcement and report publication dates, etc. Ideally meeting dates should not be altered to avoid:

a) members finding that although they could have attended on the original date they cannot make the amended date; and
b) those required to originate and submit items and reports for the Board to alter what can be complex reporting procedures.

Ideally, Board Meetings should not be cancelled, although a short postponement may on occasion be inevitable. In most companies there is routine business which needs to be authorised or considered, and cancellation may mean that required authority is not obtained, either leading to delay or possibly commitment without authorisation.

Timing and despatch of Agenda

There is no current legal requirement to generate an Agenda for Board Meetings or any prescription regarding its contents. Commercial pressures (apart from the need to be able to demonstrate to shareholders and others that proper control of the company is being undertaken) will usually dictate that all Board Meetings should be properly convened. The simplest way of effecting this is by sending a properly composed and issued Agenda with back-up data to every member in good time, so that directors are:

a) able to exercise the required control;
b) able to make informed judgements on the matters requiring decisions; and
c) have information of the current company strategy and tactics (drawn from interfacing with their colleagues) to apply to their own direct responsibilities.

It is perhaps worth emphasising that *all* directors should be sent an Agenda and supporting documentation. This should apply even when a director has indicated that he will be unable to attend and/or will be out of the country (when company law states that there is no obligation to send him an Agenda). In this way the director will receive not only the agenda but also the supporting documentation. Since most boards operate under a kind of 'continuum', with policy developing in reaction to events, by reading the documentation and the minutes, even directors who were unable to be present at a meeting should remain comprehensively briefed and updated.

Ideally, an agenda should be despatched at least seven working days prior to the meeting and be accompanied by all relevant documents. Unless this occurs many members will attend not having read the papers, leading in turn either

- to decisions being taken based on incomplete knowledge, or
- using valuable meeting time whilst individuals check points in documents only received just before or even at the meeting.

Where papers do need to be given to members late a résumé of the salient points should be requested as a covering sheet (see DATA SUBMISSION CONTROL).

Retention

There is no legal obligation to preserve Agendas but it can be helpful to keep them, particularly if proposed resolutions are incorporated, since the wording may be capable of re-use (although of course it may be preferable to refer to the minutes for the same purpose).

Ambushes and assassinations

Introduction

A responsible and supportive meeting member will avoid springing surprises on their colleagues and particularly the chairman. However a minority of members are not averse to such tactics and seek only to promote their personal aims and reputation even if this means that the aims of the meeting itself are subordinated to such personal aims. The dangers of such action are not only that the target is wrong-footed and that the meeting's aims are subordinated to personal aims, but also that revenge may be sought and the meeting's efficiency and effectiveness destroyed by individual member in-fighting.

Ambush

Ambushes can be created in several forms:

- a personal attack (which is more in the nature of an assassination – see below) on the efficiency of a meeting member or their report or assertions;
- a trap deliberately laid for the unwary;

Example

Suggesting apparent support for a project using real or imagined facts, which are later countered either by revealing them as untrue or defeating the proposal in open meeting by producing countering data. The point is that such countering data could have been made known to the target (privately and in advance) but was deliberately concealed and only used in a high-profile environment.

- by using time pressure. This device is widely used not necessarily in any malicious way although the results could be dangerous for the personal situation of other meeting members.

Example

A director arrived for a Board Meeting with a 50-page report on a fundamental matter and stated as he tabled the report: 'We need a decision on this now.' Any report of such length inevitably requires attention and may require individual meeting members to investigate the alternatives and the data presented, as well as the effects of approval. This is not something that can be done in five minutes when put under such pressure. Directors must take appropriate levels of care in the decisions they make and deciding an issue without studying the report and its implications could be held to be a dereliction of that duty.

Inevitably, there will be occasions when instant decisions must be made for sound reasons. Other than in such instances, the Chairman should seek to prevent such practices being repeated. Similarly the effect of incorporating DATA SUBMISSION CONTROLS may also seek to avoid repetition.

Defences

The nature of the ambush is such that it is unexpected and thus it is difficult to prepare for it. However, it is important to know at all times where the power of a meeting lies. Power may shift within a meeting (and can shift depending on the subject matter under consideration) but the perceptive meeting member should be able to identify where it is located. This power base is usually contained within a relatively small number of people usually including the Chairman, whose views tend to determine the decisions. If a member does not have an 'alliance', no matter how informal, with a member or members of the power base it may be difficult not only to gain acceptance of their own projects, but also should they be the subject of an ambush, there may be no support from elsewhere in the meeting.

On a more practical level, it may be advisable not so much to try to defeat the ambush (and the ambusher) as to question its validity and timeliness.

Examples: Defences

1. Query whether the item being put forward lies within the power or aegis of the meeting. If not, it should be ignored. If so, then the question of whether advance notice should have been given might also be raised.

2. Head off the attack with words such as 'I am aware of that point and have been investigating it with a view to bringing a report to

---

> our next meeting which would seem to be a more appropriate time to consider it.'
> 3. Request an adjournment or recess whilst the point is considered or additional data checked.

Essentially, what the target is doing in each case is attempting to buy time for consideration of the point made. This should be allowed by the Chairman – after all, the ambusher may have had the opportunity to consider the matter at their leisure. Obviously, if support can be evinced from other members, this would be helpful.

'Assassination'

In many ways this is a far more serious situation than an ambush, unpleasant though that may be. An ambush is usually mounted to promote a particular project or destroy the chances of success of a project which does not appeal to the ambusher. In an 'assassination' the target is not so much the project (or its destruction) as the person – that is, one of the meeting members and colleagues of the instigator. Where there has previously been antipathy the target may have some warning of the action and may be able to deflect the attack, provided some support is forthcoming from the remainder of the meeting members. Where there has been no advance warning or evidence of antipathy it may be very difficult to counter an 'assassination'. Keeping good records of meeting contributions and data submitted may be of assistance if lack of capability or contribution is being alleged.

Appraisal

Introduction

The purpose of an Appraisal (or the potentially less emotive term 'performance review') scheme is to provide an opportunity for employer and employee to meet to discuss the progress and performance of the employee since their last review session, to consider whether any shortcomings in past performance or any skills needs required by forthcoming challenges and changes affecting the organisation/employee's job can be provided by training or coaching, and to determine the priorities, training and career path for the future. Ideally, such a meeting enables both parties to determine exactly what the expectations of the other are in order to determine and assist progress. Suitable time must be allowed for the meetings which, properly organised and operated, will enhance the understanding of the parties of the others' priorities, etc. Recent research indicates that 25 per cent of employees leave within a month of an appraisal interview. Whilst it is possible that some of these are employees in the wrong position, this is such a large figure that it is likely that the reason for them leaving may be due to a poorly conducted appraisal rather than a poor appraisal.

Scheme implementation

A review of an employee's performance, particularly where the results are linked to financial reward, can be very emotive and such a process should be implemented with great care and with the benefit of a full communication process.

1. Introduction of process

Those primarily responsible for the operation of the scheme – the management – must be briefed on its aims, administration and problems, and also be trained in conducting the process and interviews.

Initially a discussion document should be distributed which will identify the main aims of the scheme. It should address:

a) the enabling of employee and manager to assess, within a structured meeting, actual performance against pre-set objectives and planned performance;

b) the establishing of strengths and weaknesses, and, from them, training needs;

c) the means by which aims and targets for the following period are to be set and measured;

d) the establishing of career paths;

e) the objective and supportive role required of the assessors;

f) the need for full communication and consultation with employees to enable the positive aspects of the scheme to be attained;

g) how the administration of the scheme will operate including the appeals procedure;

h) how the training needs identified by the discussions will be addressed;

i) determining any career path and arranging training to lead to the next one or two stages.

2. Proposals concerning format, procedure, appeal

From these initial discussions the outline scheme can be refined, certain problems and their solutions identified and the administration clarified. These points need to be codified into a guidance 'crib' for management. The scheme then needs to be communicated to and discussed with the workforce. This should fall into two parts:

a) an initial written document setting out objectives and administration, etc., of the scheme, which will give employees time to consider their concerns and questions; and

b) meetings at which employees will be able to discuss both such concerns and the scheme. It is essential that this process is as open as possible, since without the commitment of the employees to the process, it cannot work. Reassurances or guarantees regarding the maintenance of salary increases may be required, and opportunities for those with a poor review to have another chance may assist acceptability. If the scheme is to be tied to a bonus or salary review, that dimension must also be addressed. Since the latter may be contentious, there may be an advantage in not linking results to payment – at least initially.

3. Concept training

As a result of this process the scheme format may have been somewhat changed, and it may be necessary to rebrief the management. Coaching may need to be repeated, since it is essential that all those involved in carrying out interviews should attend, with the aim that within the organisation all interviews should be conducted on a similar basis and to similar criteria.

4. Pilot scheme

This will have the effect of highlighting difficulties in the scheme within the organisation, and will allow both employees and managers a chance to try the system before full implementation. The results of the pilot scheme should be publicised and explained.

The benefits of the scheme are long-term and considerable, and can only be attained if the scheme works properly, thus time spent in planning and perfecting the scheme should be a sound investment.

Paperwork

An essential tool that will enable appraisal interviews to be conducted in a constructive manner is the provision of updated paperwork. The paperwork required includes:

- a job description, which ideally should have standards or measures of performance for each task. The review of progress can then be linked to and based upon the level of attainment and, as a result, should be more objective and factual than would otherwise be the case;
- an appraisal form itself, of which two examples are shown below; and
- a procedure advising all involved how it is expected the process will be conducted.

a) At the time of each review employees will be given a performance review with a copy of their latest job description.
b) Each employee will be requested to complete Part I (self-assessment) and to give the form to their manager at least a week before the date set for the interview (which will be shown on the form).
c) The manager will consider the completed form and prepare a checklist of personal views on the self-assessment. Reference should be made to employees' Training Records for guidance on past development and possible future training.
d) In a previously arranged meeting employee and manager discuss Part I and reach agreement on the attainment rating. This may mean altering the rating in either direction. In the event of a failure to agree the appeal procedure will be used.
e) Employee and manager jointly complete Part II: priorities for following work period, and identification of any training needs.
f) All the performance appraisals for each manager's employees are discussed with a director and [personnel administration] to try to ensure a uniform approach throughout the organisation.
g) The job description should be updated (if necessary), and training that has been identified during the process should be arranged.

h) Performance review takes place every six months, although, if there is a particular need, it may be appropriate to review some employees at shorter intervals.

Organisation

Managerial/supervisory staff performance review/plan

Note

Some questions may require a commentary style answer. If space is insufficient please use a continuation sheet.

PART I Background

Name	Position
Department	Date appointed to position
PR Form issue date	Interview held

Is the job description for this position up to date and correct? If not, please specify the area(s) in which it is deficient.

If there are changes, are you able to cope with the altered responsibilities – or do you require training in order to cope?

If so, please specify what type of training

Have you since the date of your last review undertaken any training? If so, please give details, assess the worth of the training, and state how it is helping you in your job.

Is it likely that there will be changes to your responsibilities before the next Review? If so, do you feel you will be able to deal successfully with these changes, or will you require training? If so please indicate the areas where training may be necessary.

Are there any personal factors that could have an effect on your performance in the near future? If so, please provide details.

Is there any other information which you feel has a bearing on this review process and/or the performance of the job? If so, please provide details.

In the chart set out below, list the measures of performance for each of the duties set out in your Job Description and then grade your performance on a scale of A–E (A: you have always achieved the standard set in the measure, B: these standards have usually been achieved, C: sometimes achieved, D: seldom achieved, E: never achieved).

		Rating
Position Objectives	Measures of Performance	A B C D E

1. ⎤
2. ⎟
3. ⎬   (Data derived from job description)
4. ⎟
5. ⎦

If you have graded yourself D or E for any of the duties, please state for each why you feel you have performed at this level.
General

Did you achieve anything else within the period which is not covered by your job description? If so, please give details.

Was there anything you needed which would have improved your performance? If so, please give details.

Have you been able to help any colleague with his/her work? If so, please give details.

Are you able to deal with all requirements for information concerned with your job from

– superior	YES/NO	– colleagues	YES/NO
– other internal	YES/NO	– external sources	YES/NO

If the answer to any of these is NO, please state why you feel this was the case.

Do you feel you are able to get on with those with whom you come into contact?

What do you feel is (are) your main strength(s)?

What do you feel is (are) your main weaknesses?

On the scale on the previous page (i.e. A–E), how do you rate yourself for the following?

Accuracy:	Diligence:
Setting priorities:	Relationships:
Motivation:	Adaptability:
Commitment:	Overall performance:

PART II Assessment
A Performance Review interview with ....was held on .... at ....
The assessment provided by the jobholder was reviewed and the ratings confirmed/altered as shown.

The overall performance rating was agreed as .... (A–E).

PART III Priorities and training
Please set out an analysis of any action(s) agreed to be implemented, giving measures of performance and time-scales if appropriate.

1.
2. etc.
Please indicate priorities for the forthcoming period
1.
2. etc.
Please indicate any career path envisaged

Training needs: Please set out the type of training required and, if relevant, the timing of such training.

Signed   .... Jobholder
         .... Manager
         .... Date

Reviewed by .... Director .... Date ....

Organisation

Non-supervisory staff performance review and plan

PART I Background
Name   Position
Department   Date appointed to position
Issue date   Interview held

This form needs to be completed by you and handed to your supervisor/manager at least seven days before the date set for your interview (see above). Be fair to yourself and try to give honest answers to each question. Do not be afraid to write 'No', if that is the correct answer – we develop at different rates and at different times in our life. The aim of the review is to help you perform your job to the best of your ability, and, if you have the ability and so wish, to train you for your next job.

Is the job description for this position up to date and correct?

If not, please specify the area(s) in which it is out of date or incorrect.

On a grading scale of A–E (A: you have always achieved the standard set in the measure; B: you have usually achieved that standard; C: sometimes achieved it; D : seldom achieved it; E: never achieved it), mark how well you feel you performed each task on your job description.

		Rating
Position Objectives	Measures of Performance	A B C D E

1. ⎫
2. ⎪
3. ⎬   (Data derived from job description)
4. ⎪
5. ⎭

What is your overall impression of your performance of your tasks over the period since the last performance review (on a scale of A–E)?

How satisfied are you with your performance? WELL/ FAIRLY/NOT.
If you are only Fairly Satisfied or Not Satisfied, do you have any views on why this is the case?

Have you achieved anything else since the last performance review?

Was there anything you needed which would have improved your performance? If so, please give details.

What do you feel is (are) your main strength(s)?

What do you feel is (are) your main weaknesses?

Are you interested in training and progress?

Part II Assessment
A Performance Review interview with .... was held on .... at .... The assessment provided by the jobholder was reviewed and the ratings confirmed/altered as shown.

The overall performance rating was agreed as .... (A–E).

Please set out an analysis of any action(s) agreed to be implemented, giving measures of performance and time-scales if appropriate.
1.
2.
3.
4.
5.

PART III Priorities and training
Priorities for coming period

1.

2. etc.

Training needs: Please set out the type of training required and, if relevant, the timing of such training

Signed .... Jobholder

.... Manager

Reviewed by .... Director .... Date ....

The Appraisal Meeting

The paperwork suggested above provides an essential foundation for the meeting. However it is only a foundation – albeit one that provides objectively determined facts which should avoid the meeting degenerating into a 'yes you did/no I didn't' confrontation.

The purpose of management is to help people succeed. This may be stating the obvious and yet experience indicates it is a concept more normally overlooked than complied with. Appraisal depends on a dialogue between employee and manager, and whilst it should commence with a review of the past, essentially it should concentrate on the future – identifying challenges in order to generate requirements for training (which can then be fed into the training plan). The objectives to be set for attainment during the period to the next review:

a) need to be real objectives, having point and relevance to the job in hand;

b) need to be capable of attainment within the period, or, if not, the fact must be recognised and a realistic time-frame set; and above all

c) need to be joint objectives, agreed and accepted by the employee – unless this is so, there will be no commitment to their attainment, and hence little chance of success.

The reviewing manager will need to prepare for the interview both by reading and considering the self-assessment form and by completing the following checklist. The checklist should be completed with total objectivity outside the structure of the interview, and exists as an information prompt during the interview – comments can thus be backed by fact, derived from checking the situation, rather than from opinion.

Performance review and plan   Reviewer's guidance
Subject name   Position
Before completing this checklist ensure that the background
information shown on the subject's form is correct and the Job
Description referred to is the current issue.

1. If the information given by the subject is incorrect, state the
   discrepancies.
2. If you disagree with the grading of work by the subject, state the
   reasons.
3. If you disagree with the overall assessment, state the reasons.
4. If the items listed as achievements have been incorrectly stated,
   note corrections.
5. Are suggested training needs acceptable? If not, state the reasons
   or alternatives.
6. Career path – is there a path for this employee? If so, suggest
   timing and training required, if not, suggest alternative solution(s).
7. Would a further review before the next performance review is due
   be helpful? If so, suggest a date.

The meeting is <u>not an opportunity to repeat criticism</u> of <u>past performance</u> –
if performance was poor then that should have been dealt with at the time.
Obviously, if despite previous support, guidance and warnings poor performance continues, that will need to be discussed from the point of view
of investigating whether there is any way in which the employer can provide support, etc. The meeting <u>must look forward rather than backward</u> and
attempt to discover the way forward and what is needed to ensure progress.
The meeting must be kept secure from interruptions. If it is constantly interrupted by telephone callers and/or visitors, the message being given to the
employee is: 'You and your future are not as important as these other matters.' This may, in some case, be true, but conveying it helps no one and will
merely serve to demotivate the employee during a process one aim of
which is motivational.

360° appraisal

In recent years the concept of 'all-round' appraisal has begun to be more
widely used. This entails not simply downwards-only appraisal (that is,
input from the person to whom the employee reports) but also input from
those who report to them (if any), their colleagues and those above them –
both immediately and one or two links in the command chain removed.

29

The advantage of this type of appraisal is that it can develop into a far more objective view of the subject and usually results in improved communication mainly since very often motives have been misunderstood (that is, the motivation is not necessarily wrong, simply misconstrued). The disadvantages are:

a) with everyone it involves more time;
b) with the subject, it can, unless everyone involved restricts their comments to constructive aspects, resemble a 'witch-hunt'.

Obviously, the latter needs to be guarded against since otherwise the whole point of the scheme is lost.

It may be helpful if an external consultant, experienced in dealing with such schemes and the fallout therefrom, is available to guide those who feel 'damaged' by some of the comments.

The propensity to issue hurtful comments is to some extent lessened when the originator realises that whilst this time they are the instigator of comment, the next time they could be the subject.

Case study:	*Full circle*
	Northern Electric introduced 360° appraisal in its Human Resources (HR) Department as part of a process seeking to address the changes needed in the role of corporate personnel following a major restructuring of the business.
	Each member of the HR team sought views from their colleagues, subordinates and seniors. These were collated independently and fed back to the subject by the external facilitator. Most managers found the 'most enlightening aspect' of the whole exercise was noting the differences in the perceptions of their actions, attitudes and behaviour between themselves and those with whom they interacted. The results were improved communication, greater involvement of all colleagues and departmental members and better delegation and devolvement of authority at all levels.

> **Note**
>
> Recruitment Agency Office Angels conducted a survey in early 2000 and highlighted the tendency for many employees to leave within a short time of their first appraisal. The survey concluded that if this occurred, it was usually the result of the interview being conducted improperly. The main problems were:
>
> - postponing the interview thus making the employee increasingly anxious;
> - interviews being suspended by constant interruptions;
> - the rationale behind the systems seeming to be confrontational and critical rather than constructive and supportive;
> - managers not familiar with the employees concerned having to stand in to conduct the interview;
> - the whole process being very rushed.

feed beck - v. important. - better relationships
└ influence   \into. |
| direction
Productivity

Bad news

Introduction

Almost inevitably meetings will need to be called from time to time to convey bad news. Where such communication is required externally the suggestions made under CRISIS COMMUNICATION meetings are appropriate. Where, however, the news is related to internal considerations (perhaps the most obvious being a requirement to lose employees via redundancy – which is used below to illustrate the matters required to be addressed during the meetings which should follow such a decision), although it may be necessary to consider the external implications, the main considerations needing attention are internal and specifically with those personally affected. It is important to realise that in such a situation everyone is concerned – both those who are to go and those who are to stay. Whatever the nature of the bad news where it affects the other party, ideally the person responsible for communicating the news should attempt to visualise himself in the position of the respondent and ask the question: 'If that was me:

- What would I want to know?
- How would I like to be told?
- How would I like to be treated?

Background to bad news – a redundancy

Whilst it should be the aim of every employer at all times to maintain full employment for all employees, since it is impossible to forecast product demand at all times, it is also impossible to guarantee full employment. No employer should ever guarantee that there will be no redundancies. Few people are gullible enough to believe that such promises are unlikely to be broken. When promises are broken the effect is to damage the credibility of those that made them as well as the guarantee itself. It is far more sensible to adopt a redundancy policy. Legally, employers who make more than twenty employees redundant within a period of ninety days need to meet in order to consult their elected representatives as well as them as individuals. It may minimise the emotive reactions that may result once redundancies are required if mentioned at a time when there is no need of them, if

a) a comprehensive redundancy policy is agreed;

b) meetings unconstrained by time considerations are held with all involved; and

c) elected representatives are consulted.

The draft procedure set out in the following checklist could be used as a base for action. This is important since in following the various steps, meetings and discussions which are essential in such circumstances will be required to take place – and to be evidenced as having taken place. The advantage of adopting such a policy is that it will act as a criterion for carrying out the communication/meeting requirements which are an implicit part of the process. However, it is important for those convening the meetings both with elected representatives (who may or may not be personally involved) and with those who are selected, that they are treated with

- courtesy and as equals;
- an appreciation of the very real difficulties many people will face as a result of the decision;
- an appreciation that for the majority of employees work is a social occurrence as well as a means of earning a living and breaking their employment means the breaking of relationships and friendships which may be an important part of their lives. This is often overlooked by employers and as a result when meetings are held where comments are made without appreciation of susceptibilities, antagonism can be created where formerly there was only sadness and resignation. This is important not only for those affected by a termination, but also for those who will remain, the sustaining of whose morale is essential for the continuation of the business in changed circumstances and with a reduced number of employees.

A policy – and a procedure to be followed

In the following policy not only are the various matters to be addressed set out, but in a number of cases the policy/procedure itself throws up a requirement for meetings. If these are adhered to experience indicates that many of the difficulties to some extent inherent in such a process will be overcome.

Checklist

1. Prepare a policy wording which covers all the items set out below. Ensure it is made readily available to and accepted by all employees.   *Consult with employees*
2. Agree who are to be the employee representatives – ideally with deputies in case the elected representatives leave.

3. When a reduction in employee numbers seems likely, meet and advise all employees that this situation is likely to arise and redundancies are anticipated. *Consult with employees*

Note

This is not notification of actual redundancy but an indication that this could arise. With the benefit of consultation and communication the ideas and suggestions of those with most to lose can be generated which may avoid the need to cut jobs.

---

4. If trade unions are recognised, then consultation must take place with them for set consultation periods. These periods are ninety days if 100 employees or more are to be made redundant over a period of ninety days at a single establishment, or thirty days if ten or more employees are to be made redundant over a period of thirty days. The Department of Employment must also be notified. (Note: Where there are recognised Trades Unions their elected shop stewards must be the elected representatives with whom the employer must consult.) *Consult with representatives*

5. Elected representatives will be consulted via meetings regarding the extent of the redundancies, its reason, the proposed method of selection for redundancy, terms, etc.
Consult with representatives

6. The basis of selection must be fair and objective to all involved.

7. Individual performance (absenteeism, attitude, disciplinary record, etc.) can be taken into account provided that all records are suitably and objectively scrutinised.

8. Employees will be invited to volunteer for redundancy, making it clear that the requirement to retain suitable skills to run the operation may result in some offers being rejected.

9. All employees volunteering will be seen individually and if selected will be given a letter confirming the fact and the amounts payable on their termination (including redundancy amount, wages and holiday pay to leaving date, any payment in lieu of notice should the full statutory or contractual, if longer, notice not be given, less any reductions for loans, etc., repayable to the employer).
Consult with employees

10. Once the required number of job reductions has been agreed and the number of voluntary redundancies is known, jobs – and the jobholders – to make up the difference must be identified.

11. Individual consultation will take place with those selected.

Alternative suggestions made by those selected will be
considered.   *Consult with individuals*

12. The staffing of the whole organisation will be examined for
    any vacancies which some of those selected for redundancy
    might be able to fill. (Note: It is essential that the possibility
    of alternative work, to save redundancies, is constantly
    examined and possibilities discussed with those whose jobs are
    at risk.)

13 If alternative work is found for an employee, confirmation of such
    alternative work should be given to the employee with an
    indication of the length of a trial period, during which notice for
    termination due to redundancy will be suspended.
                                              Consult with employees

14. The redundancy payment will be calculated in accordance with
    the State Scheme [for example] save that there will be a minimum
    payment equal to two weeks pay, all years of service will count,
    there will be no upper maximum on a week's pay, and the
    amount will be increased by 50 per cent.

15. For employees nearing retirement, any enhanced redundancy
    payment will be restricted to the amount of gross pay they would
    have received between the expiry of their notice period and their
    normal retirement date.

16. All redundant employees will have available the employer's
    outplacement service which will attempt to help employees to
    consider their options and to find alternative positions.
                                              Consultation available

Terms

Immediately an employee knows they could or are to lose their job as a
result of redundancy they tend to have two immediate questions:

a) How long do they have in service before they will be required to leave?
   and

b) How much will they be entitled to in compensation.

Obviously, such information must be provided at the first meeting with
those selected after the consultation process in terms of decision and selection has been completed. However, since such data can be difficult to
remember, particularly in what can be a somewhat traumatic interview, it
is essential that full written details setting out all options and entitlements
are given to those selected immediately that they are told, and that some
named source of answers to the questions that may arise from time to time
is provided. Clear, honest information and communication can help defuse

much of the antipathy that may otherwise be generated. Most people are quite capable of accepting and coping with bad news – even the loss of their job. What they resent is not being given full information or being treated as being incapable of appreciating the reality of the situation. Statements about the situation should be given using straightforward, honest English – trying to 'soften' bad news by the use of euphemisms and jargon does not make the truth less palatable, it merely adds insult to injury by implying that the subject can be patronised. If it is thought that it would assist individuals, counselling services could be provided.

Outplacement

Increasingly, organisations making employees redundant realise the moral obligation they have to such employees and attempt to provide facilities to help them find alternative jobs. If this can be refined and advertised, then it should provide some reassurance to those affected that assistance is available. Outplacement can range from the provision of a written guide to seeking and interviewing for another job, to convening meetings to provide full career guidance, rewriting career histories and CVs and even head hunting on behalf of those affected. Constant discussions, consultations, etc. are required.

There may be tasks the organisation will require to be done on a bought-in basis which might be sourced by redundant employees acting in a 'self-employed' capacity. Those selected should be invited to consider such possibilities and to attend meetings to discuss them. Assistance given to redundant employees to start their own businesses may be not only well received by those directly affected but provide a clear message to all concerned regarding the attitude of the company to its responsibilities.

Aftermath

Inevitably, the greatest attention needs to be given to those who are to lose their jobs. However those who remain also need as much as information as can be given to them and should also have the opportunity to attend BRIEFING GROUPS and be given as much information as possible about the current and anticipated situation. However, reassurance regarding future employment prospects, which will understandably concern many, should only be provided where it is completely safe to do so and if given should be limited to a set period.

Those remaining often experience feelings of guilt that they were not chosen to be made redundant and these feelings will need to be countered.

General guidance

Basically, the more thought that can be given to the problems in advance of the need for action, the more likely the organisation is to be able to deal productively with all the questions and difficulties that will be experienced. Trying to deal with such problems without time to consider all the ramifications, or more commonly trying to evade so dealing, is likely to lead to have disastrous consequences.

Doasyouwouldbedoneby

Redundancy has been used as an example of bad news requiring meetings and consultation on a continuing basis to be communicated – not least since it is an occurrence which is all too frequent nowadays. However, the principles of developing a policy/procedure in advance and of ensuring that it is adhered to at the time applies to all instances where bad news is to be communicated. The principle of 'doasyouwouldbedoneby' (from Charles Kingsley's *The Water Babies*) is perhaps a sound criterion. If the person who is responsible for running these meetings can imagine themselves as the other party and tailor their comments, attitude and response as if they were the one receiving rather than giving the bad news, this may help achieve an understanding of how the other party feels and is likely to respond during and after meetings, etc. Attempting to see matters as the other party is likely to see them and to visualise their responses may be the first step to constructive communication in such circumstances. However, if the news is really totally unexpected, the recipient may be unable to comprehend anything else (even details of payments and benefits) for some time, by which time the meeting may have ended. This may be true even though it seems to the party giving the news that they are absorbing what is being said. Their eyes may seem to be alert, but vision and hearing may actually have switched off whilst the brain races to assimilate all the implications of the news. In redundancy the most common immediate reaction is panic at the thought of the ongoing bills and costs and how these will be faced without an income. In realisation of this some employers have made the announcement on a Friday, provided written data at that stage and invited employees to discuss the situation the following Monday, by which time they assume the realities of the situation may have sunk in and the employees may be more able to absorb information and ask meaningful questions. (There is a counter-argument that this leaves 48 hours without explanation or support which is a long time for concerns to multiply.)

The difficulty of absorbing the news in such situations is the whole rationale behind the legal obligation to consult employees in such a situation – most of us take time to generate a considered response. Equally, most people need an opportunity to discuss the situation and the implications. Ample meeting time must be allowed for this purpose.

Board Meetings

Introduction

Whilst the main purpose of this section is to provide guidance for those attending meetings of the directors of limited liability companies, the principles apply to most meetings of most executive committees (that is, those of decision-making and controlling bodies) of most organisations. As far as limited liability companies are concerned control is exercised by their Boards of Directors – even though the shareholders own the company, the directors run it on their behalf and shareholders have no right to interfere (their only course of action would be to remove the directors). Currently there is no explicit obligation for a Board to meet, although their authority is needed to approve the accounts, recommend a dividend and to convene the AGM, so at least one meeting each year is necessary. Under proposed EU legislation, a Board of a PLC would be required to meet at least four times each year and to consider certain prescribed business. In practice, most Boards tend to meet rarely in anything approaching formality but far more often informally. Directors have a duty to act with due care and attention. Failing to meet regularly could be argued to be a failure of this duty. If this were held then they could be made liable for loss, etc.

Administration

In LTD and PLC companies the responsibility for convening, running and recording the decisions of the Board is usually that of the Company SECRETARY. Those responsibilities include:

a) generating an AGENDA in liaison with the Chairman and convening the meeting in good time;

b) ensuring the required QUORUM is present before the meeting can commence;

c) taking, reporting and recording any apologies for absence;

d) ensuring that any notifiable interests of directors are noted where these might affect voting (or even attendance) on items likely to be discussed at the meeting. Directors are required to advise the company of any personal interest they have in a third party with whom the company trades or has a relationship. Directors are required to deal at arm's length with third parties and the existence of a personal involvement of a director (or their spouse or minor children, that is, 'connected persons') with a third party could lead to a conflict of interests. Disclosing the interest alerts the company to the potential conflict. The details should be recorded (and updated should they change) and the effect checked with the Articles of Association of the company. Requirements vary from interests being allowed to the directors being restricted regarding:

- taking part in discussions of the subject items,
- voting on the matter,
- being required to disclose and/or account for any profit made,
- being counted as part of the quorum of the meeting;

e) checking members have all the documents required;

f) having available spare documents in case members have mislaid or forgotten them;

g) ensuring those matters that support the meeting – refreshments, note-taking aids, protection against interruption, and so on, are arranged;

h) ensuring the meeting adheres to and does not overlook any item on the agenda;

i) ensuring those who speak and vote are entitled to do so (this relates to the question of directors' interests and may require a tactful word to the Chairman at the appropriate time);

j) ensuring the appropriate voting power is reflected when votes are taken;

k) ensuring that meeting's decisions are clear and clearly understood by all present;

l) noting the sense of the meeting in the MINUTES;

m) keeping the minutes secure and available to members;

n) ensuring action is effected as required by the meeting and reported on at the appropriate time.

Attendance and apologies

Directors have a legal obligation to attend Board Meetings. An Agenda must be sent to them all – other than those who it is known will be abroad on the date of the meeting. However, it may be administratively more convenient to ignore this relaxation, particularly where papers and data are sent with the Agenda, since, even though they may not be present, directors will still wish (and need) to be updated on results, solvency, data, reports, etc.

Under Table A of the Companies Act 1985, should a director fail to attend

Board Meetings for six months or more without due cause, their colleagues may remove them from office. For this reason it may be important to record who is present at each meeting – and thus who is absent. Equally, those who are absent should be expected to account for their absence and if the reason is acceptable, it would be advisable to record this in the minutes. Some companies and other organisations require those present to sign an attendance book.

Composition

A meeting's length tends to be proportionate to the number of people present. If that number is inflated by persons with no right of attendance and/or whose contribution is unnecessary, the effectiveness of the meeting may be diluted and its duration prolonged. Effective contributions that are concise yet comprehensive should be actively encouraged. Setting a time-limit on the meeting – or on individual items – may encourage this and should avoid time being wasted on trivia.

Reports, etc., should accompany the Agenda or a note regarding late submission be appended. Tabling at the meeting, or a bulky or complex report, should be avoided – decision-taking on its contents is likely to be uninformed. If this is unavoidable then a brief précis of findings and/or recommendations should always be included. Data should be assembled in agenda order.

Although the degree of formality of the meeting will differ widely according to company custom, it is usual for all members to sign a book of attendance, and to address and speak through the Chairman. Decisions reflect the collective responsibility doctrine of Board work and the Chairman should summarise arguments, before taking the 'sense' or decision of the meeting – usually by consensus, but occasionally by vote.

In a Board Meeting each person entitled to be present has a right to be heard on each subject. The guidelines set out in DATA SUBMISSION CONTROL may be helpful to improve meeting efficiency.

Preparation

It is perhaps stating the obvious to suggest that those attending Board Meetings should be prepared for them. However, experience suggests that at times and for some people it does seem that little time has been spent in preparation. For directors of limited liability companies this obligation is implicit in company law. They have a duty of care, and failing to prepare for a meeting of a decision-making body for which they are responsible must be a breach of that duty. At the very least preparation will entail reading all the papers and reports sent with the Agenda and at the most will be the preparation demanded of the Chairman to be familiar with every aspect of every item under consideration. Preparation could thus include:

Checklist

1. Reading the minutes of the previous meeting and actioning anything required at that meeting.
2. Reading the reports issued with the Agenda (and other reports impinging on the subject matter to be considered at the meeting).
3. Making investigations as a result of questions which arise from the reports in 2.
4. Discussing with colleagues aspects of items arising under 2 and 3 (and anything else that has occurred since the previous meeting which should be dealt with at the meeting).
5. Commissioning investigations into aspects arising from these reports or other matters and either requiring or writing a REPORT on such matters.
6. Checking statistics, facts, etc., quoted by or referred to in reports from other members (unless the sources are considered impeccable).
7. If presenting material, a report, etc., either attempt to pre-empt questions by including data in the item or attempt to consider all the questions least welcome – and some convincing answers.
8. (If acting as Secretary) Ensuring there are copies of reports, etc. that will be discussed in case members have omitted to bring theirs. Update and have available any records that are required to be signed/initialled during the meeting (e.g. Attendance book, file copy of last Minutes, Register of Seals, etc.). Arrange security of room (see below) and refreshments etc.

And so on.

Decision-taking

Board Meetings exist to take decisions. This does not necessarily involve change as some decisions may be of the 'keep it moving exactly the way it is' type, nevertheless progress has been reviewed and a decision taken. It is the duty of the Chairman to ensure not only that decisions are taken, but that before that stage is reached, an opportunity is taken to hear everyone on the matter and hopefully achieve consensus. Every director has a right to be heard on every item, although equally reality and pressure of time will encourage all members to be concise and brief.

Few Boards resort to voting on each item and generally matters are approved by a unanimity of approach or attitude. This places a burden on the Chairman to ensure that everyone has a chance to have their say. Where there is a lack of unanimity, a vote may need to be taken to ensure that the voting strength not only prevails but is seen and recorded as prevailing.

Good chairmanship, with clear personal and meeting aims, drive and personality, are essential to the success of the meeting. It may be helpful if the Chairman understands the likely views of the individual members before the discussion. If it is obvious that an item has little support the amount of time devoted to it at the meeting may be curtailed in favour of more extensive examination of items where opinion is evenly divided and where an in-depth discussion is essential. Whilst the Chairman will want to keep the meeting moving in order to deal with all its business within the time allotted, discussions of salient matters must not be truncated. This may mean that the members need to be coached in how to put their arguments and points across in a cogent manner and with a minimum of repetition or deviation.

Decision recording

Company law requires MINUTES of the meetings of shareholders and directors of limited liability companies to be taken and preserved safely. Minutes should record the decisions taken and not the arguments for and against the decision or any commentary. They should be full enough to enable a third party to understand the decisions taken and yet brief so that their clarity is preserved. Ideally, a draft of the minutes should be given to each director and they should have an opportunity to correct any wording that they feel is incorrect. Once a version has been agreed as the accurate record of the meeting, the Chairman should sign and date them. If this procedure is followed the minutes usually become conclusive evidence of the proceedings. Normally minutes are compiled from notes or even tape-recordings taken at the meeting. Once a set has been approved and signed, the notes may be best destroyed. Drafts of minutes are often changed before approval but the signed set is the approved version. Under discovery rules such notes could be required to be produced. If these were different from the final version a challenge to the approved version might be mounted.

Security

The security of the meeting should be preserved. Whilst this inevitably means that discussions in a meeting should be both confidential and protected from eavesdroppers, it also means that members should respect the need by instructing their staff not to interrupt the meeting for anything short of an emergency. The meeting room should be located in a quiet area and not have a phone or at least have the capability to bar all incoming calls. A suitable method of summoning those required to attend part only of the meeting (e.g. to deliver a report) should be arranged.

Brainstorming

Introduction

Most meetings covered by sections in this book are of a more formal nature where the event follows its convening by an Agenda so that the items to be covered by the discussions are known in advance – and members have a chance to prepare for the items requiring decision. At the opposite end of the spectrum of meetings is the entirely unstructured encounter where the members may have a question or problem to be addressed and are simply challenged to provide a solution. This is brainstorming, which can be used in a variety of instances although is perhaps most widely used within the creative field.

Approach

The concept of allowing – even encouraging – meeting members to develop a discussion which veers off at tangents to the original problem or proposition seems to strike at the whole logic of a meeting in terms of attempting to ensure that decisions are efficiently produced in a cost-effective manner. However, if the time factor is controlled (e.g. by imposing an overall time limit on the session) brainstorming sessions can themselves be productive, albeit in an entirely unforeseen way – which is of course the rationale for the whole process.

Case study: *Bare necessity*

Pacific Power and Light is an American power supply company, which operates in some harsh conditions in the north-west USA. In many of the mountainous areas power is transmitted via overhead lines which often break under the weight of accumulated ice formed by the freezing of the constant snow. The method of avoiding the line breaking was to send linesmen along the line with long poles constantly knocking the snow off before it froze. This was laborious and dangerous and not entirely effective over long periods. Several brainstorming sessions with the linesmen were held to try to solve this problem, during one of which a linesman complained that the previous week he had been chased by a bear. The suggestion was then made that if they could get the bears to climb the poles the weight of the animals would shake the snow off the lines and thus avoid the problem. Out of this developed a further suggestion that if they put honey pots on top of the poles, that would induce the bears to climb the poles in the first place. The problem of how to place the honey pots on top of the pole then arose and the use of a helicopter was suggested. Cutting across this fanciful and increasingly risible idea came the notion that the down draft from the helicopter rotors would itself remove the snow before it froze. Nowadays Pacific Power & Light use the down drafts from overflying helicopters to clear their lines.

Key technique:

Perhaps only a few companies would have allowed a meeting of their staff, addressing the serious problem of change, to apparently go off on the fanciful tangent of encouraging bears to go after honey pots at the top of power poles, and yet it was only because they had gone through that idea that the eventual solution was discovered.

Downside

This case study is a classic example of a serious problem being solved by means of an unstructured discussion, which is unlikely to have been allowed within a formal meeting constrained by an Agenda. The essential ingredient is spontaneity, with ideas that even those voicing them would not have thought of without a trigger generated by the unstructured discussion. The danger with brainstorming sessions (and a factor common to most other meetings) is that they can be hijacked by the articulate or self-assured to the exclusion or detriment of those less able to express themselves, although possessed of valuable and original thought. It is important that this does not occur since many of those who are unable to express themselves well may have a wealth of ideas which are not expressed simply because they lack the opportunity to put their ideas forward.

Drawing out such ideas is a challenge for and places an onus on the leader or facilitator to ensure the full participation of all present, curbing the excesses of some and encouraging others. Conversely, should the Chairman's preferences veer towards the opinion of the articulate members, then there may be a tendency 'not to hear' any opposition or alternative ideas. Thus the Chairman will be manipulating the meeting, and, although those opposing may be able to muster an attack and make their points known, if the Chairman is not in favour of their views, it may be difficult to win the arguments, and further, impossible, without the Chairman's support, to succeed in any implementation. This negates the whole concept of brainstorming, which is that every idea should at least be considered for a brief time before it:

- generates a new idea or concept which can be considered in turn;
- is discarded as untenable;
- is adopted.

Recording ideas

Because a brainstorming session is unstructured, this should not imply that the essential aspect of recording what took place at a formal meeting should not occur. Ideas are ephemeral and can be forgotten almost as swiftly as they arose. Ideas discarded along the route to the ultimate and adopted concept may have value elsewhere. For this reason some informal (but comprehensive) jottings of such notions may be useful – if only to act as a base (or 'pump primer') for the next brainstorming session.

Training sessions

Brainstorming, or a similar approach, can be used within training sessions, where, although the facilitator may be working within a structure, the delegates themselves have only broadest outline of the programme.

Case study: *Doubts resolved*

Pfizer UK recently introduced management training aimed at converting corporate values (including concepts such as 'respect for people', 'customer focus', 'leadership' and 'teamwork') into measurable actions. The management training sessions had three aims:

a) to help delegates understand their own strengths and weaknesses;
b) to learn how to address problems not by buck-passing or blaming a third party but by asking themselves how they could improve; and
c) by creating means by which their behaviour could be measured.

One sceptic of the whole process – both aim and process – recalled how at the end of the first gruelling day, the external facilitator suggested one last exercise. He objected and stated that he had had enough. Rather than either agreeing with him or not, the facilitator suggested the other members continued without him. When the sceptic hesitated (basically torn between admitting failure and leaving, or being perceived to be weak and staying – in either event losing face) the facilitator asked the other members what they felt. They all responded by giving reasons why they felt he should stay. This taught him how dependent he was on his colleagues' good opinion and how much they valued him. In turn it also demonstrated how essential it was that he should have similar feelings for his colleagues – and thus the point of the corporate values the training session was attempting to validate.

Introduction

The Confederation of British Industry stated during the early 1990s that the greatest challenge of the following decade would be for employers to communicate with their employees. In the early years of the twenty-first century that perhaps remains the greatest challenge and one which, if research is to be relied upon, seems a more complex challenge, and one that is less rather than more effectively being taken up. Research also indicates that communication within smaller organisations (i.e. those employing 100 or less) is actually worse than that in larger organisations. With smaller organisations it should be possible for those in senior positions not only to know their employees individually, but also to communicate with (that is, talk to and above all listen to) them. Inevitably with larger organisations this is likely to be more difficult, and rather than one-to-one sessions it may be necessary to use briefing groups to disseminate information and to start the communication process.

Title

In this section the word 'briefing' is used to describe any meeting of up to (say) 40–50 employees coming together with their manager or a more senior manager to discuss work-related items. Such groups may be known as 'task forces', 'updating sessions', 'team meetings', 'quality circles', and so on. The title is irrelevant, since the underlying purpose of each – *to allow/generate communication on matters of interest to all involved* – is virtually the same.

Briefings fall into three main types:

a) team meetings where the composition is only the team who work together normally (e.g. the Payroll Department) and the subject matter is their work and the problems directly related thereto;

b) cascade briefings where the audience is the work team but the subject matter may comprise more general issues than their work-related items; and

c) management briefings where employees (possibly from more than one

49

department may be gathered together and) are updated for a specific purpose, by a senior manager.

To a considerable extent all such devices can be termed 'meetings to foster an investment in people'. Formal rules are not required to be able to invest in people, although the Investors in People (IIP) initiative cannot be faulted. Quoted in the CBI's *Corporate Communicators Handbook* (Kogan Page, 1997) are the following statistics from organisations introducing IIP:

a) A chemist increased its operating margins from 7 per cent to 11 per cent.
b) A stationer saw a 41 per cent increase in profits and a 40 per cent reduction in labour turnover in two years.
c) A manufacturer saved 60 per cent on purchases and improved customer spend by 200 per cent.
d) A firm of solicitors improved their net profit by 45 per cent.
e) A borough council reduced manpower by 13 per cent whilst achieving higher service levels.
f) A building group reduced accidents by 50 per cent.

Team meetings

These are the most favoured type of briefing since the subjects discussed tend to be of direct interest to the employees – their own work and problems and difficulties related thereto. Since the interface is usually with their immediate superior, they are also less likely to be deterred from speaking out. In all kinds of briefing the input of the leader is essential, but this may be more of a challenge for leaders of team meetings since they may be supervisors untrained and inexperienced in giving PRESENTATIONS. To ensure effectiveness, all those who will be expected to run such sessions should be given coaching whilst the guidance set out in the following checklist may also be of assistance.

Checklist

1. Monthly meeting led by the supervisor/manager attempting to be as informal as possible.
2. Team leader needs to prepare by:
   - listing problems for team consideration;
   - considering suggestions made;
   - arranging for a team member to take notes and to have these available at subsequent meetings;
   - having available company briefing;
3. Team leader must ensure all questions are raised and noted, and answered either during the meeting or subsequently if the

information is not immediately available. (Note that answers will be provided unless this would breach confidentiality, in which case this will be stated.)

4. Team leader should ensure sufficient time is allowed for discussion of items. Meetings will not normally last more than 30–45 (or less than 15) minutes.

Team leader preparation:

1. Collect news from own and other departments (arrange exchange with team leaders from linked departments).
2. (If linked with cascade briefing – see below) familiarise yourself with the content of the company briefing obtaining answers to anticipated questions.
3. Collect suggestions made from those in the team, consider objectively, list problems and advantages but do not prejudge – let team discuss and come to its own conclusion(s).
4. Check that all questions raised at previous meeting have been answered and, if not, obtain/prepare answers for team.
5. List all items for consideration in a checklist for reference during the meeting to ensure nothing is overlooked.

Running the meeting:

1. Three essentials: preparation, preparation, preparation!
2. Remember that the meeting is purely a conversation such as you might have at the workplace. Try not to be nervous – it should be an informal chat with the aim of trying to understand each others' viewpoints, problems and aims.
3. Forget about yourself – concentrate on the business you want to get through (from your checklist) and ensure team members have a fair hearing.
4. Be enthusiastic – only if you are will the team be.
5. Encourage all to participate. If certain members are shy or not forthcoming, try to involve them by asking whether they agree or disagree with items. Some employees will speak automatically but others may require encouragement. Help those who have difficulty expressing themselves by putting a version of what you think they are saying in your own words and then checking with them that you have it right.
6. Stress that although the team welcomes the opportunity to deal with complaints, it is not just an opportunity for a grumble session. Suggest that anyone with a complaint should also be prepared to put forward a solution – the discussion can then be steered to the positive aspect of solution rather than the negative aspect of complaint.

7. Don't imply that all problems have immediate answers, or that the suggested answers can be implemented, or that the team should always have an answer. If there is a question without an answer, refer back to line management to try to find the answer and let the team know this at the next meeting.
8. Summarise the discussion and decisions before closing the meeting. Ensure any members who have been asked to carry out tasks know this.
9. Set the date for the next briefing
10. If asked to cancel the team briefing meeting: DON'T.

Note

If it is absolutely impossible to hold the briefing at the date/time stated, then postpone it by no more than two working days, but never cancel even if there seems little to discuss. The success of this communication dialogue depends upon the regularity of the meetings, and cancellation will destroy trust in the system and thus the concept itself: the impression will be given that the process is unimportant. If there is little to discuss then keep the meeting short. Remember that, in any case, you will have the company briefing to refer to, and that this, in turn, may generate comment and/or question.

Cascade briefing

The principle of cascade briefing (advocated by the Industrial Society for many years) is that the people with the ultimate responsibility for generating employee communication are senior management. This is indisputable. However, the idea of cascade briefing then goes on to suggest that information should cascade through the organisation like water flowing downhill as in the following illustration.

Using the cascade process senior management brief middle management who brief junior management who brief supervision who brief employees. Whilst this may be fine in principle, it can founder if not introduced properly if a number of suppositions prove false.

The process assumes that all those doing the briefing are:

a) committed to the principle;
b) able and willing to brief adequately (giving a PRESENTATION is reckoned to be one of the top ten most stressful undertakings);
c) able to answer the questions that the briefing session will generate; and
d) prepared to remove all barriers to the disclosure of information.

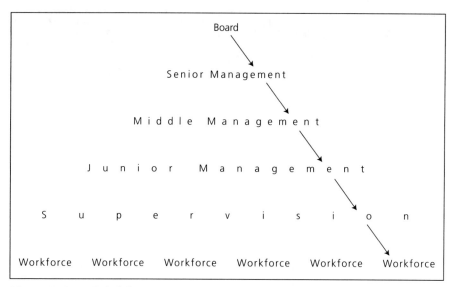

Figure 1 Cascade briefing

These four assumptions are unfortunately unlikely to be valid in some organisations for the following reasons:

a) There can be a resistance from some managers to both the principle and practice. This needs to be overcome. However, forcing someone to carry out a procedure will not necessarily ensure that it is carried out effectively.

b) Few people are natural communicators and messages can become distorted either because the speaker does not necessarily understand the matter fully or cannot deliver the message in a clear way, that is, in terms capable of being understood by the audience.

c) Some managers hoard information (for self-aggrandisement or preservation of power reasons) and dislike passing it on.

d) Where the subject matter is particularly complex and not fully understood by the briefer it is very unlikely that they will be able to answer questions which are an important part – in many respects the essential part – of the briefing process. Faced with questions they could either try to bluff their way out or admit ignorance and need to refer back. This the briefer may feel is a reflection on them, that is, they may feel that having to say 'I don't know' undermines their authority.

Major problem

The foregoing overlooks what is perhaps the most major problem of the whole process – the fact that messages can be misconstrued in repetition.

Case study: *Chinese whispers*

Number One felt that the organisation needed a boost to its morale and addressed all the senior managers stressing the fact that there were new orders to be won, which would ensure the factories worked to capacity for at least a year. One of the aims of the address was to reassure everyone that there was no question of short-time working or losing reliable employees through redundancy. The request was to pass the message on 'right through the whole company'.

The senior managers went away and saw the middle and junior managers. The message the latter heard, however, was 'We've got an awful lot to do in the next year, so get everyone cracking on it – only the reliable are safe.'

In turn the junior managers saw their supervisors and passed them the message that 'we really need to crack down on everything for the next twelve months.'

The supervisors, some of whom were having discipline problems, saw this as an opportunity and told their employees: 'Unless you lot pull your fingers out and improve productivity you'll all be out of jobs by the end of the year.'

The trade union representatives were extremely concerned that redundancies might be in the offing and immediately requested a meeting with the Chief Executive at which they threatened a work-to-rule unless the full facts were put before them.

Key technique:

Making oneself understood can be difficult at the best of times but when one's message needs to be passed through several intermediaries, almost inevitably they will be misinterpreted, misconstrued and/or misunderstood. It is generally accepted that each time a message is passed on between 15 per cent and 25 per cent of the true meaning is lost. Unfortunately, this does not mean the message simply becomes shorter. Whilst this would not be ideal, at least 75 per cent of the message might get through. What can occur is that inaccurate or imprecise data and/or opinions are substituted for the 'missing message' passages in order to make up something similar to the original volume.

If this were not serious enough at least it assumes that the parties who misconstrued the message genuinely wished to pass it on. In some cases those involved may deliberately distort or suppress part or all of the message.

The above case study is based on a real-life event (albeit somewhat exaggerated for effect) and encapsulates the classic problem of a confident message emanating from the chief executive being translated and mangled in repetition until it reached the ears of its intended audience in a form almost exactly the opposite of that intended. Even with the utmost commitment to the truth, it is difficult to repeat to another other than the simplest message in the way intended by the originator. This simple truth reflects the inherent danger of cascade briefings. However, it can be made even worse since delegating communication empowers those down the line with the opportunity should they wish to filter and skew the message. In addition, any feedback or return messages also run the risk of being mangled in repetition, if not similarly filtered.

If Number One cannot speak personally and widely (and consistently) to those at the sharp end then a message must be consigned to paper and distributed. Even then, the words used should be examined carefully for unwanted undertones or misinterpretations. Simple language needs to be used; any use of jargon or words not in everyday use can confuse and mar the effectiveness of the message.

Pushing water uphill

Each of the problems highlighted above can be overcome to a large extent by adequate training, which itself underlines the necessity for any such procedure to be introduced only after all involved have received training in making presentations and dealing with questions outside their spheres of knowledge. This in turn, however, discloses another problem – that a cascade briefing's greatest value – that of disseminating information to a large number of people in a short space of time by using the management chain of authority – is also its greatest weakness since the process will inevitably generate questions and there needs to be a 'reverse cascade' by which such questions can 'flow up' to the Board and answers can 'flow back'. Even where such a process is set up, some managers may filter out questions that

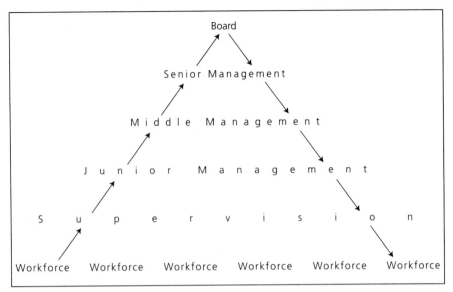

Figure 2   Reverse cascade briefing

they feel may reflect badly on themselves or concern matters they do not want discussed. It should be easy to get water to flow downhill – it is almost impossible to get it to flow uphill yet the whole point of briefing is to do just that. A one-way flow is not communication – it is merely information. To generate communication we need a two-way flow.

Setting up an effective 'reverse cascade' can work although part of the problem is that it can take so long for answers to come full circle, via the 'downhill' cascade, that the point of the questions may be lost. Indeed, it may create so great a logistical problem that it may be preferable to appoint one senior manager to carry out all the briefings on a regular basis, rather than use the cascade principle.

Senior manager briefing

This has a number of advantages:

- the quality of the various briefings is more likely to be equal;
- the briefings themselves may gain in prestige by being conducted by a senior manager or director;
- by virtue of the manager's seniority they should have personal access to all information which should allow them to answer most of the questions posed and can revert back individually to those to which they have no immediate answer.

Conversely, the fact that the briefings are being conducted by a senior manager may stifle some contributions. Great care needs to be taken to preserve the authority of the intervening management. However, experience indicates that those managers that undertake such a process, whilst it is time-consuming, discover a great deal (not all good) about their organisations and their employees. The process should also demonstrate to the employees the genuine interest of senior management which may have a beneficial effect on morale and commitment.

The brief

Regardless of whether cascade or direct senior management briefings are being used (and even in some cases where team briefings are in operation) the process of dissemination of information can be aided by the preparation of a regular management brief giving salient facts to act as a record of what was discussed and as a spur to discussion.

Example

Organisation   Briefing sheet ref. number.........
Date prepared   Briefing to be completed by (date)

1. Company position
    To (date of subject period) sales are .... [up] on budget, profits are .... [up] on budget.

2. Orders
    The order book is satisfactory with .... weeks' orders in house
    Special information (general news of particular orders, special interest, etc.)

3. Promotional activity
    News of product developments, new launches reactions, advertising campaigns

4. Production information – productive units achieved compared with budget, downtime, lost time, quality – achieved and problems. Anticipated demand in productive terms, etc.

5. Personnel information – system changes. New state requirements, etc.

6. Health and safety matters

7. Other general information

8. Contacts for further information/answers to questions raised at previous briefings

---

Best practice audit

Boards cannot afford to assume that practices (such as regular briefing sessions), which they wish their managers to adopt, are being implemented, so a regular check on how well the company is doing in terms of briefing its employees may be advisable. The questions set out here may provide a base to determine whether communication is effective and briefings are working – and, on a far wider scale, whether employment relationships are adequate, which may be the most important question capable of being addressed by regular briefing meetings.

Checklist

1. Have we devised plans and discussed their implementation with employees so that the employees themselves 'own' the plans in order to gain their active commitment to them?
2. Do we encourage employees to make suggestions and constructive criticism about the organisation, its products, procedures and endeavours?
3. Is there mutual respect between management and employees and are the pressures on employees in terms of working and private lives balanced?
4. Does management listen actively to employees (and vice versa) on every occasion so that the full facts and implications of all matters are exposed?
5. Are initiatives introduced via consultation and agreement thereby generating a 'yes' reaction and a genuine commitment?
6. Does everyone involved realise that as part of a single team their objective is to satisfy their customers in order to achieve the aims of the organisation?
7. Is training provided and are employees encouraged to develop their skills and talents at all times?
8. Do managers and employees work in job-related teams mutually helping solve problems, meeting output targets that they have agreed?
9. Is there an open culture whereby information flows both ways thus generating genuine two-way communication – and is this situation confirmed by the employees?
10. Are employees proud to state that they work for the organisation?

Warning

All briefings are PRESENTATIONS and as such those required to give a briefing should refer to that section – particularly in terms of using visual aids.

Briefing the Chairman

Introduction

For routine meetings the Chairman's own preparation (see BOARD MEETINGS and CHAIRING MEETINGS) may be sufficient to equip them to deal with the meeting, particularly if they know the meeting members and thus know how they are likely to react to the various items of business. However, whilst many Chairmen will be sufficiently experienced and aware to be able to deal effectively with such meetings, inevitably some are not and new Chairmen may welcome briefing notes, even if these are used more as a back-up aide rather than as an 'on-the-spot' script or crib.

This is particularly important at more formal meetings where most of those present will not be known to the Chairman and certain legal formalities must be processed in a set fashion.

The Chairman's crib

For more formal meetings (e.g. a company's Annual General Meeting), particularly where there are legal requirements with which compliance is essential, it may be helpful in advance of the meeting to generate a crib or script which the Chairman can follow.

Example

At (time) call meeting to order with a few introductory remarks such as...

'Ladies and Gentlemen I welcome you to the ..th AGM of .... Ltd/plc. I will now start the formal proceedings, following the conclusion of which you will be able to meet members of the Board and other executives and chat informally over some refreshments. We have, as you can see around you, provided displays of our products and services and I hope you will find these of interest.

The Notice of this meeting was despatched to all members of the Company on (date) and I will ask the Secretary to read it.

(Secretary reads notice.)
The first item on the Agenda concerns the consideration of the directors' report with the report and accounts for the (twelve) months ended (date). Those accounts and the Balance Sheet as at that date have been audited by your auditors Messrs (Name) and I request Mr/Ms (name) a partner of that firm of registered auditors to deliver their Audit report.

(Auditor reads report.)
May I propose that the Report of the Directors, together with the annexed statement of the Company's accounts for the (twelve) months ended and the Balance Sheet as at that date duly audited be now received and adopted?

Has anyone any questions or comment? *(Pause)*
(If questions are raised it will be necessary to deal with them or if they are of a technical/financial nature pass them to Finance Director to handle.)

Following on from your consideration of the report and accounts may I also propose that a final dividend of (amount) per cent or (amount) pence per share on the Ordinary shares of the Company payable on (date) be now declared for the (twelve) months ended (date)? I call upon (name) to second these proposals.

All those in favour please raise your hands. *(pause)* Anyone against? *(pause)* *(Assess and declare result.)*

I therefore declare the motion carried.

Item 2 concerns the re-election of the retiring director(s). The director(s) retiring by rotation is/are (name) and I have much pleasure in proposing that (name) be and he hereby is re-elected a director of the Company. I will ask (name) to second that proposal.
All those in favour? *(pause)* And against? *(pause)* *(Declare result.)*
I declare Mr (name) duly re-elected a director of the company.

Note

If more than one director retires by rotation, separate proposals are required for each unless a proposal to deal with all such re-elections as a single entity is first passed by the meeting. Proposals may also be needed to re-elect any directors who have been appointed since the previous AGM. Re-elected directors may wish to express their thanks to the meeting.

Item 3 concerns the re-election of Messrs (auditors) as Auditors of the company and I call upon Mr (name) to propose that resolution and Mr (name) to second it.

All those in favour? (*pause*) Anyone against? (*pause*) (*Declare result.*)

Item 4 authorises the directors to fix the remuneration of the Auditors and I will ask Mr (name) to propose that resolution and Mr (name) to second it.

All those in favour? (*pause*). Anyone against? (*pause*) (*Declare result.*)

Is there any other ordinary business for consideration?

(Note

Other than the proposal of a vote of thanks to the Chairman/Board it is unlikely that anything else can be discussed by the meeting since notice of such business will not have been given (unless of course every shareholder entitled to be present is present and agrees to waive notice).)

I therefore declare this xxth AGM closed. Thank you.'

Additional reference notes:

1. Legally, the shareholders can only receive the report of the directors and the accounts. Even if they reject both, those items remain as they are and need to be filed with the Registrar.
2. The shareholders can only approve or reduce the final dividend recommended by the directors. If the directors feel that a recommended final dividend is likely to be reduced then it may be preferable to consider paying a second interim dividend (which does not need shareholder approval).

Extraordinary General Meetings

By its very nature (that is, not being 'ordinary' and thus fairly uncontroversial) it is more likely that business at EGMs can provoke disagreement and dissent. This is even more likely to be the case should the company get into difficulties and unpalatable measures need to be proposed. The following draft is a condensed version of a brief developed for the Chairman of an EGM of a company that was in serious financial trouble and where the former Chairman and Managing Director had been forced to resign to allow a capital restructuring to be put in place to try to save the company.

The EGM having been properly convened the former Chairman then submitted an item for consideration by the meeting. This item was submitted too late for inclusion in the agenda in the notice of the meeting. However, rather than risk the need to convene a further EGM the Chairman requested the meeting (at which all members were present) to allow consideration of the matter (which it did) although the proposal was then voted down. It was fortunate that all members were present, as, had less than 95 per cent been present and thus able to waive notice of the item, it is unlikely if it could have been properly put to the meeting.

Example

[Mr Chairman – I have assumed that voting will be by show of hands in which case a simple majority of hands carries the resolution – that is, each shareholder has one vote. It is, however, possible under the Articles for any shareholder to demand a poll in which case the meeting must be suspended whilst we conduct a poll where the number of shares held will decide the outcome. If a poll is demanded we also need to appoint tellers. I have prepared three sets of voting slips in case polls are required.

I have primed several shareholders so that each time you ask for a seconder you should always find someone ready to second your proposal.

I have prepared a handout which details all the Resolutions and Proposals to be placed before the meeting (including a résumé of the additional matter put forward for consideration by Mr K) and will give one to each member as they arrive. This should make it easy for them to follow the business as it proceeds.

Call meeting to order at 12 noon.]

CHAIRMAN: 'Gentlemen, my name is [x]. At a meeting held on 4 February, the Board requested me to assume the role of Chairman. This Extraordinary General Meeting was convened by the Board by a notice issued on 28 January which I propose we take as read – does anyone object to that?'
[*Pause – then, assuming no objection...*]
'Subsequently a shareholder holding in excess of 10 per cent of the shares, as stipulated by the Articles, requested that a further item of business be considered at this meeting and we shall deal with that later. Since the first item on the Agenda concerns myself I shall vacate the chair and ask Mr Y to deal with this item.'

RESOLUTION 1 – Confirmation of appointment of 'Chairman'

Y: 'Thank you, Mr Chairman. Gentlemen, as you will see the first item on the Agenda concerns the proposal to confirm the appointment as Chairman of Mr X. Neither this nor items 2 and 3 need shareholder approval nor to be dealt with at a General Meeting, but in view of the financial situation of the company and the dissent that has prefaced this meeting, it was thought this would be advisable. Accordingly I would like to propose that Mr X's appointment as Chairman of the Board be and it hereby is confirmed. Do I have a seconder? All those in favour? Anyone against? I declare the motion carried and hand the meeting back to the Chairman.'

RESOLUTION 2 – Confirmation of appointment of Managing Director

CHAIRMAN: 'Thank you. At the meeting which appointed me as Chairman, a majority of the directors also appointed Z as Managing Director. I would now like to propose that Z's appointment as Managing Director be and it hereby is confirmed. Do I have a seconder? All those in favour? Anyone against? I declare the motion carried.'

RESOLUTION 3 – Confirmation of appointment of Secretary

CHAIRMAN: 'The directors also requested Mr Y to assume the role of Company Secretary in addition to acting as a non-executive director and I would like to propose that Mr Y's appointment as Company Secretary be and it hereby is confirmed. Do I have a seconder? All those in favour? Anyone against? I declare the motion carried.'

RESOLUTION 4 – Creation of additional share capital – alteration to Memorandum

'The next two items on the Agenda concern the creation of additional share capital which is necessary so that the major restructuring of the company on which we have been urgently working for some weeks can take place. Copies of the formal resolution, which must be filed with the Registrar of Companies, have been given to you and I would now like to propose

THAT the share capital of the company be increased from £10,000 to £2,000,000 by the creation of:

a) 990,000 new ordinary shares of £1 each ranking in all respects *pari passu* with the 10,000 existing ordinary shares of £1 of the company,

AND

b) the creation of 1,000,000 Cumulative Redeemable Convertible Preference Shares of £1.

The notice refers to a coupon rate of 10 per cent, but on reflection the Board feels that the rate needs to be left for individual negotiation. Does anyone object to this?

[*Assuming no one objects and having canvassed all the shareholders and found that no one currently does, the motion itself can then be put to the meeting.*]

'Do I have a seconder? All those in favour? Anyone against? I therefore declare that resolution carried.'

RESOLUTION 5 – Change of auditors

[I have checked with the retiring auditors who have no objection to making way for the new auditors. They have confirmed that with the steps currently being taken by the Board, including the matters that are to be dealt with later in the meeting, they have no intention of lodging any statement requesting that any matters be brought to the attention of the shareholders.]

'Your Board originally requested ABC to act as auditors, a role they carried out until the end of 199x, when it was felt more advisable to appoint auditors located nearer to the company. Messrs ABC have indicated their willingness to resign. As part of the investigation carried out by Mr Z, an audit-type investigation on the activities of the company to 31 December 199X was completed by Messrs DEF, and I now propose that Messrs DEF be and they hereby are appointed auditors of the company until the conclusion of the first Annual General Meeting which must be held within the next few weeks. Do I have a seconder? All those in favour? Anyone against? I declare that resolution carried.

RESOLUTION 6 – Company strategy

'The next item concerns the restructuring of the company and the strategy for the next two years, details of which are included in a report from Mr Z copies of which have been sent to you. This report, and the 'audit' report contained within it, were prepared very urgently and within a very short time span. Inevitably, some shortcuts have needed to be taken and the Board is aware that there are a number of errors which need to be rectified at an operational level. We are asking today for shareholder approval in principle to the plan which requires amongst other things, the conversion of shareholder loans which we will deal with in a moment.

I would like you to confirm your acceptance of this plan with those comments in mind, and without discussion since the matter is so urgent we need to move to the next item. However if any shareholder does wish to make any comments...

[You will have to play this by ear. Since all the shareholders have already received a copy and we have spoken to several and dealt with a number of their queries, this may go through 'on the nod' – which is hardly surprising bearing in mind the pressure evinced by the shareholders to nominate Mr Z as the replacement MD. You can expect Mr K to object of course but unless he can be specific and concise I suggest you request him to put his comments in writing for the attention of the Board when it comes to implement the plan. In any event, and as I am sure Mr K knows, the voting strength is overwhelmingly in favour of acceptance.]

RESOLUTION 7 – Conversion of loans made by shareholders into share capital
'The next item concerns the conversion of loans made by us all to the company as part of our shareholding investment. Although it may be arguable that it is permissible for such loans to be counted as shareholders' investments, the advice the Board now has, including that from its new auditors, is that these loans do not constitute part of the shareholders' investment and that if their total is excluded from that category, the company is insolvent and should not continue trading. We need everyone to agree today to convert these loans into ordinary shares, and unless this is done, we cannot see that new money can flow into the company which is the only way the company can survive. Thus the directors view this matter as a question of 'convert loans into shares or decide to put the company into receivership'. If the loans are not converted your investment is lost, whereas if they are converted, there is a chance of saving the company and thus your investment. This is not something on which we can vote since it must be an individual decision, although one where everyone's money rests on everyone agreeing to convert. I must stress that as one of the largest investors and, in terms of my shareholder loan, largest creditors of the company I am prepared to convert my loan into shares immediately after this meeting. Any comments?'
[Again you will have to play it by ear. I have forms that will enable shareholders either to:

a) convert loans into ordinary shares, or
b) convert some loan into shares and some into Cumulative Redeemable Convertible Preference Shares (CRCPS), or
c) invest new money in Ordinary shares and/or CRCPS.

You will need to try to insist that before people leave they sign a form.]

RESOLUTION 8 – Item put forward by Mr K
'The last item concerns a request made by Mr K for an alteration to the

Articles. Before we can consider the item itself (which we have set out on the Handout) you will note that the short notice given in respect of this item needs to be agreed. The Board think it would be advisable for everyone to agree to consider the item and thus I would propose that proposal (8) be considered by the meeting notwithstanding that short notice was given. Those in favour? Any against? I declare the motion carried in which case we may now deal with the proposal put forward by Mr K that the Articles of Association be changed as set out in the wording of the resolution. Mr K do you wish to make any comments regarding this resolution?

[Again you will have to play it by ear but at the end of any discussion, you may like to comment – the Board's view being entirely against the proposal – and will need to put it to the vote – in favour, against, declare result. I suppose it is just possible that we might have a demand for a poll here, although my canvassing indicates little support for a proposal that really could have the effect of restricting the actions of the Board in its efforts to save the company.

If there is any argument, you could make the point that the chance of saving the company is slim and it may be that the only way forward is to transfer ownership of part or all of the company which would almost certainly mean the offer of additional shares. Since no existing shareholder is willing to put more money into the company it is difficult to see the point of the proposal.]

That concludes the business of this Extraordinary General Meeting – may I thank you for attending.'

Additional reference notes:

1. As stated in the script prepared for the Chairman the confirmation of the appointments of Chairman, Managing Director and Secretary are not matters that need to be presented to the shareholders and this course was adopted only to try to test and gain support for the actions of the new Board in a difficult situation.
2. The question of issuing convertible preference shares with a variable coupon rate requires legal advice. In fact here, against the advice of a number of people involved, it was put to and approved by the meeting, although the issue was never actually implemented.
3. The value of canvassing support, particularly in difficult situations

like these, cannot be overemphasised. Whilst not wishing to stifle fair criticism and comment, the will of the majority needs to prevail (subject to ensuring there is no oppression of minority rights) and the company must be moved forward.

4. Using a handout, particularly as here where there was an extra item of contentious business, should aid attention, and the flow of the meeting.

5. The preparation of such a script/advice, and the canvassing of support, took several hours but since the meeting went without a hitch the aim was achieved. The concept was to try to pre-empt every alternative, or to provide an answer for every possibility.

Researching likely outcomes

Briefing the Chairman should not be restricted to providing a 'script' not least since many Chairmen will be able to operate entirely without such support. The person charged with the task (usually the Secretary of the meeting) should also consider each item of business and be prepared to provide a view of the likely support/opposition for these items in case it is necessary to canvass support from the uncommitted or to attempt to deflect the antagonism of opponents. This is particularly the case with formal and external meetings (e.g. the General Meeting covered previously in this section where the power resides with shareholders who may be anything but a homogeneous entity – comprising many different facets quite likely to coalesce with some on some matters only to splinter from such groups on others). With internal meetings the ideal is consensus but where this is impossible canvassing or checking support and opposition seems a logical method of preparing for the event – and a suitable precaution against the Chairman's position being left exposed.

For less formal meetings, such briefing might be restricted to advising of any likely reactions to particular items of business.

Cabals, cannibals and confrontations

Introduction

Meetings, regardless of the organisation involved, involve the interfacing of people who may be drawn from a variety of backgrounds and cultures. Almost inevitably this will mean that whilst there may be unanimity on a majority of items of business, on some there may be antipathy and even downright opposition. In addition some people are incapable of sublimating their personal preferences and prejudices in the interests of the body being governed and thus personal views may override organisational requirements. Finally, some meeting members are political animals quite capable of 'doing a deal' whereby in return for support for a colleague's pet project, they will expect support for theirs – either current or anticipated. Whilst not recommending the processes referred to below, there is no doubt most will be encountered from time to time and meeting members would be wise to recognise the tactic, even if in some cases there may be little they can do to combat the effects.

Cabals

One of the most widely known meetings is that of the weekly UK Cabinet. The government actually comprises far more ministers than the twenty or so who form the Cabinet, which is thus an 'inner core', the composition and size of which is designed to try to ensure swift progress. This manner of working started under Charles II, who after the restoration of the monarchy wished to move away from the previous method of government by an over-large Privy Council and preferred to use a small body of just five trusted advisers. The initials of these advisers were C A B A L which later came to form a word 'cabal'. In turn, the word cabal has come to mean a secretive part of a larger whole. The word 'cabinet' comes from the French word for a small private room in which, presumably, the six persons of King and 'cabal' could be accommodated easily. The possibility of the existence of a cabal within the larger body must not be overlooked, or unsuspecting members, not privy to the separate deliberations of the cabal, may find themselves ambushed. Indeed it is not too long ago that a British Prime Minister found herself ambushed in a similar way.

The Prime Minister in question was Margaret Thatcher, who found her support in the Cabinet and party insufficient for her to continue in office. Not that this kind of experience was new to her. As John Campbell in his book *Edward Heath – A Biography* (Cape, 1993) records, when Margaret Thatcher was a minister in Edward Heath's Cabinet, the animosity between the two led Heath to position her at the far end of the cabinet table and on the same side as himself. Eye contact was thus impossible and it was said that Heath never asked for her views, except at the end of a discussion when he was shuffling his papers ready to move to the next item on the agenda. To counter this sometimes Mrs Thatcher would request another member to raise business for her, trying to outmanipulate the manipulator.

Cabals have considerable power particularly if they include the Chairman. After all, if two or three members consistently side or support the Chairman there is in existence a power bloc which it will take considerable opposition to defeat. Whilst not advocating the creation of a cabal, there is no doubt that at times it can be effective, particularly in working towards a predetermined outcome.

Cannibals

Inherent in predetermining an outcome is a requirement to consider the means by which such an outcome can be achieved. In trying to move towards this outcome the Chairman, or indeed any other member since all may have pet projects to broach for approval, must consider the realities of the situation. In most committees, business needs the support of a bare majority of the members to gain approval. However, experience indicates many members tend to forget this basic point or think, alternatively, that the more forcibly they argue, or the louder they demand, very often the more chance of success. This is a little like one of Aesop's Fables in which the sun and the wind vie to make a traveller remove his overcoat. The wind uses all the forceful power at its disposal but the effect is only to make the traveller draw his coat ever closer round his body. The sun simply shines, and swiftly the traveller removes his coat, persuasion being better than force. Nowhere is this perhaps more demonstrably the case than in the United Kingdom. There is a facet of the British personality that determines that the more one shouts and raves, or even uses force, the less likely is one likely to succeed. In addition it is dangerous to assume that one will always be dealing with reasonable people. If other meeting members are determined to gain information or to move to a particular outcome, they may be prepared to use any tactics to hand in order to achieve their ends. The only counter that can be used is to try to form an alliance with other like-minded members and thus form a 'bloc' through which objections are more likely to be taken into account than would be the case if raised by a sole member.

Neutralising the opposition

This does not imply that those wishing to promote certain items of business should bring in the heavies, it is merely a recognition that in order to win the 'bare majority' for attainment of the outcome, taking out an adverse vote can be a valuable ploy. In determining the outcome and considering methods of moving to that position, the experienced meeting member must consider the opposition and identify ways of overcoming a combined position as separate entities. Obviously it is not always the case that all those identified as potentially against the item will have the same attitudes or reactions, or even feel equally strongly about it. Whilst it may be impossible to shift some members to a position of support, handled correctly or appropriately, others may be capable of being moved to a position of neutrality. Neutralising some of the opposition can be as valuable as winning support. After all, if the meeting consists of six members and the subject proposer has assessed that two colleagues will be in favour whereas three will be against, all he has to do is to neutralise one of the opposition and he can carry the day. Rather than wasting time on those unlikely to be moved, he should concentrate his efforts on the one he feels he can neutralise.

How this can be effected will depend upon the circumstances, but in a long-running committee or Board, there are bound to be occasions when the lines of battle contain different members. D who finds himself against A and B and is considering neutralising C on this occasion may find himself with B and C and against A, E and F the next time around. Agreeing to support C on another matter in return for his abstaining on the matter in hand is not only sensible from D's point of view but is part and parcel of meeting tactics. (See OUTFLANKING THE OPPOSITION.)

Confrontation

Normally, meetings proceed smoothly with efficiency and achievement if there has been adequate preparation and planning. Occasionally, however, business is required to be discussed which raises strong feelings, polarises attitudes and, if allowed to continue, can result in outright confrontation. In such a situation it is all too easy for tempers to be lost and what would normally be a rational discussion to degenerate into a heated argument, in which case carefully prepared and cogently argued cases are abandoned and a slanging match may develop. In this kind of situation it is essential for the Chairman to assert control and call the proceedings to a halt, either temporarily, that is for a recess of, say, 15 minutes, or more permanently, that is, until a later date. Requiring parties to break off the encounter should give everyone a chance to cool down and for their normal tolerance and good humour to be reasserted. It may also provide an opportunity for emissaries to visit both camps to test the possibility of some kind of mutually acceptable compromise.

Checklist

1. Remain calm at all times. Once two tempers clash then it is unlikely that any consensus will emerge, and the situation will almost certainly degenerate.
2. Note facts or opposing views without immediately commenting. Commenting hastily may merely inflame the situation, whilst the longer the member, or more than one member, can talk without being challenged, the more they may be able to reduce the pressure they feel. It is essential to try to ensure they speak separately and wait, without interrupting, until the other has finished.
3. Keep the member(s) talking and explaining the cause of the temper loss, whilst asking neutral questions to try and uncover as much of the case, or cause of concern, as possible may help, simply from the genuine interest being evinced.
4. Attempt to relax the members by means of refreshment, allowing smoking, or even declaring a recess or adjournment. Care should be taken not to denigrate the concern or infer that the dispute is not serious. The purpose of adjournment is to allow time for reconsideration, or thinking time, and not to stifle the matter.
5. The provision of refreshments, thereby diverting attention to a neutral act, may provide valuable calming time.
6. On resumption or after the initial flow has ceased, if no adjournment has proved possible, re-checking and correcting the facts as already discovered and noted. This should enable a more accurate résumé of the dispute to be prepared. Further, since time will have passed since the original outburst, a more objective view may be obtained. This process can be built upon by the Chairman questioning suspect facts or opinions, and challenging suppositions and claims where these appear to be unsubstantiated.
7. Leave as much time as possible for the calming process. Points 1–5 may require as much as 30–40 minutes. Indeed the longer the time taken the better as the more likely it is that the temper may subside.
8. If an adjournment is possible, this should give the Chairman time to investigate the case.

9. In making a decision under pressure, care should be taken to avoid setting precedents and thus decisions should be of an interim nature pending final clarification and/or approval.
10. If an interim decision is implemented, a date and time should be set for review of the matter and implementation of a final decision.

Capability

Introduction

Section 98 of the Employment Rights Act 1996 sets out five reasons for potentially fair dismissals: 1) conduct, 2) redundancy, 3) contravening a duty or restriction under a Parliamentary Act, 4) 'some other substantial reason' (which, purely for example, could include dismissal for a poor absence record) and 5) capability. Many employers find determining the last reason in the list is one of the most vexing and difficult to deal with, and any meetings held to try to pin down any lack of capability extremely difficult, not least since unless there is adequate preparation, any discussion of the problem can degenerate into an exchange of irreconcilable views within an atmosphere that can rapidly become heated.

Identifying what is required

It is perhaps stating the obvious to say that before criticising an employee for not performing a job to the standard required, etc., there should be agreement concerning what is required (although hearing tribunal cases reveals that this is exactly what some employers fail to do). The agreement of job descriptions ideally with measures of performance linked to each task is an essential foundation. Similarly the application form (to indicate any claimed skills/experience), as well as any performance review or appraisal assessment, should also be considered. Similarly the organisation needs to determine who is responsible for what:

Example: Policy

Responsibility of management:

1. to ensure there are clear job descriptions with expectations (measures of performance);
2. to ensure that all employees who are assessed for capability know what is expected of them;

3. to ensure there is adequate and meaningful communication (i.e. a two-way dialogue);
4. to ensure appropriate INDUCTION and follow-up training for employees with mentoring where applicable;
5. to ensure standards of work are established and monitored and agreed achievable targets are set;
6. to offer informal counselling and guidance (with formal counselling/coaching/training as required);
7. to ensure all employees are treated fairly and equally in terms of expectation and measurement, etc.;
8. to provide reasonable assistance, aid and equipment where employees are disabled;
9. to ensure the capability procedure is applied fairly and accurately;
10. to commit to a process of continuous training for employees so that they are able to maximise their talents and skills for mutual benefit.

Responsibility of employees:

1. to achieve the level of work agreed with a reasonable level of commitment and motivation (within a reasonable time);
2. to seek assistance if there are difficulties achieving this aim;
3. to co-operate with management in all respects in attempting to achieve the required level/quality of work;
4. to discuss with management, problems and related difficulties which could be affecting capability, in order to agree a means whereby such problems can be eradicated;
5. to take part in all discussions of the problem and all coaching and training agreed as a means of rectifying the shortcoming;
6 to take reasonable steps to maintain and improve their talents and skills.

Obviously, such a policy statement goes somewhat further than dealing with a lack of capability – the advantage may be that it stresses the positive achievements that can be derived from such investigations rather than the negative and disciplinary results that can emanate from a lack of commitment to achieve what is required.

Criteria

Capability needs to be judged by reference to certain criteria, for example:

• skill

- ability
- health and
- qualifications.

In terms of health, the onus is on the employer to ensure that any low or non-performance is not related to poor health – particularly any pressure resulting from the workplace. There have been a number of cases where employees have been able to claim compensation from their employers for stress in the workplace. Instituting capability investigation in such circumstances could be dangerous.

Qualifications investigations can be covered by means of checking claims with the appropriate authorities – for example, professional bodies where membership is claimed, previous employers where there was in-company training, and so on.

This leaves 'skill' and 'ability', where assessment can be somewhat subjective. However, objectivity may be improved by using the agreed measures of performance in the job description (JD) as a criterion and stating by how great a degree the employee is missing the level required, or simply by means of a memo setting out the required level of performance for the next, say, one or three months.

These relatively short periods are suggested quite deliberately since:

a) if there is a question of capability it is in neither party's interests for the situation to be unduly prolonged;

b) constant reassessment will then keep the problem under focus and may prompt action sooner rather than later.

In the same way that the safest application of the DISCIPLINARY INTERVIEW procedure is by measured and considered steps, so too is the requirement in dealing with a perceived lack of capability. However, here the problem is more likely to be one of omission rather than commission. In addition, the employer must be reasonable and ensure that suitable assistance is provided to the employee (training, coaching, etc.) to assist him to reach the required standard. Of course, should the employee demand training at a level where it would appear from the application form that such a level had previously been obtained, this could legitimately raise a question of false claims. If admitted, the disciplinary procedure could be implemented.

A performance improvement procedure

Discussions regarding capability or the failure to reach certain standards are not automatically disciplinary matters, and it may be preferable, rather than using the disciplinary procedure, to use a customised procedure.

Example – Procedure

1. The [employer] believes that it is in the best interests of both employer and employees for the latter to perform to the best of their abilities.
2. To assist employees attain a performance level commensurate with their abilities and its requirements, the employer will provide suitable, job-related training as identified through the regular appraisal procedure.
3. No employee will be forced to undertake training or to perform at a level above that at which they are comfortable.
4. Every encouragement will be given to those attempting to improve their performance. Where an employee wants to try to perform at a higher level, a guarantee can be provided that, should they be unable to perform at that level, they can revert to their previous position without criticism or detriment.
5. Where a manager feels that an employee is not performing to a level already required by the job, they will use the following procedure to attempt to rectify the position:
    a) Determine whether the employee is aware of the level of performance required and, if not, advise the employee accordingly allowing them a suitable time (as agreed between the parties) to try to achieve the required levels.
    b) Assuming the levels are either already known, or advised as set out under a) above, discuss the position with the employee with the aim of identifying any problems which can be resolved so that performance can be improved (this could include additional training, ongoing support, provision of instant assistance when required etc.).
    c) In liaison with the employee set a reasonable time within which an improvement is expected and arrange a further monitoring session at the conclusion of that time.
    d) Unless it is obvious that performance has improved, hold the review meeting and reconsider the problem, if necessary offering to provide more support, training etc., to enable the employee to achieve the required levels.
    e) Repeat c) and d) until the required level of performance is achieved or until the expiry of what is considered to be sufficient time for improvement.
    f) Should there be no improvement after e), or should it be considered at an earlier stage that the employee is simply not making an effort to achieve the required levels, then the matter will become disciplinary and be dealt with under the disciplinary policy.

The application of this procedure requires there to be a number of meetings. None is envisaged as being disciplinary, but since if there is no improvement the matter may become disciplinary it would be wise to treat them as if they were – at least in terms of the administration (i.e. so that there is a detailed record of what was said, agreed, disputed, etc.).

Checklist

1. Set up the discussion by means of a written note to the employee outlining the subject matter (copy to employee file).
2. Note the starting and finishing times and date of the sessions in the record of each.
3. Make notes of everything said at the sessions, including any reasons or excuses stated by the employee. (Note: As for disciplinary matters the notes should be made contemporaneously even to the extent that whatever is agreed between the parties should be noted as it is said.)
4. Confirm in writing to the employee what has been agreed and what is required for action, the timetable and date of following review (copy to employee file). It may be helpful to send a copy of a précis of the notes of record of the session to the employee stating that unless he has any corrections to lodge, within a set time – say two working days – this will form the record of the meeting.

With this kind of record it should be difficult at the next session, assuming there has been no improvement, for the employee to challenge the record, and the items that were agreed to be addressed. Ideally, the improvements required should be both attainable within the time-limit allowed, and quantifiable.

Using this approach the employer will start a pattern which if all stages have been passed without improvement (or where there is earlier suspicion that the employee is not trying) can become disciplinary.

Recording the action required

Whether the discussions are disciplinary or performance improvement-oriented, what is needed is an indication to the employee of any dissatisfaction with their performance. In communicating this to the employee at a capability review meeting it is essential that the message is clear and unmistakable. If a comment is made which is not clear, then the employee may be able to challenge later whether guidance was given.

> **Case study:** *Safety first*
>
> In a case concerning a dismissal as a result of delays caused by an employee exercising what he viewed as a safe working practice, the employers made great play of the fact that they had warned the employee previously that he was working too slowly and/or ineffectively. However, he was able to convince the tribunal that the occasions when he agreed he had been spoken to, it had been more in the nature of minor concern rather than an essential need for action – and he had acted accordingly. As a result the employers could not prove that the final 'working slowly' accusation was 'the last straw' and was not linked to safety considerations and so lost the case. (It hardly helped their case that there was little or no documentation evidencing the appointment and the requirements of the job.)

If a comment is made (even ambiguously) which is backed up by a written record, then the fact that it has been committed to writing should of itself indicate the seriousness with which the employer views the matter. Obviously, if no progress is made the sequence of paperwork itself is evidence of the attempts made to improve matters. This could be invaluable if the matter needs to be transferred for action as a disciplinary matter.

> ### Example: Meeting minutes
>
> Résumé of meeting between [manager] and [employee] held on [date] at [time]
>
> [Manager] explained to [employee] that he had been recruited as a trained order process clerk with several years' experience in companies within the industry but that since he did not seem able to attain the levels of orders processed by others in the department, it seemed he lacked sufficient experience.
>
> [Employee] explained that he was unsure of the internal procedures. [Manager] queried exactly what he meant by this and when it was explained stated that he was surprised since he had spent a day with [employee, mentor, training manager, etc.] going through the systems as part of his induction process. However he would arrange for [Supervisor] to go through all the processes again to familiarise

[employee] with them. He would arrange for this to be carried out by [date].

In the meantime he requested that [employee] attain the [targets set]. [Employee] thought these targets were achievable.

Meeting closed at [time]

Copies: File; [Employee] with note requesting any queries or corrections to be lodged with manager by [date]

Obviously, if there were no improvement a further meeting would need to be held and this point made and a further set of notes generated – a process which might need repeating two or three times. This may take time and it is appreciated that in the meantime (in the example given) the employer is paying an experienced clerk's salary for what seems to be an inexperienced clerk and obtaining a minimum of output in response to considerable input from three employees – the clerk, the supervisor and the manager himself. However, what is being achieved is either the progress of the clerk to an acceptable level, or the building of evidence that will enable the clerk to be safely disciplined in due course. This is important since the limit for unfair dismissal is now £50,000 and the employer would want to have as sound a defence as possible if ultimately the decision is to dismiss. If the employee disagrees at any stage with conclusions it would be as well to allow an appeal (as would be the case were the disciplinary procedure being used). Any appeal should be heard by someone not involved previously.

Incompetent employees

There is an obligation where an employee is perceived to be incompetent (and particularly had they been promoted by the employer to their present position) to provide training, coaching and help, and to allow sufficient time for the employee to 'grow' into the job – or, as envisaged in the Performance Improvement policy a chance for them to revert to their old position. It is unlikely that a dismissal of a newly promoted employee on grounds of incapability would be considered fair, unless there had been open review meetings and support could be shown to have been given, etc.

Chairing meetings

Introduction

No matter how egalitarian an organisation wishes to be, someone needs to take the chair at meetings – of the executive, subcommittees, of the Board or of owners' (shareholders') meetings. Depending upon the detail set out in the authority under which the meeting operates, those who take the chair may have strict guidelines within which they are required to operate or may have a wider remit which may require them to generate their own guidelines. Both pose problems. The situation regarding the status of the Chairman also needs to be checked. Most Chairmen of Boards of Directors are appointed under the Articles as 'Chairman for the time being' and thus could be replaced by another should their colleagues so decide. Alternatively some appointments are for a set period or rotate amongst the members (e.g. each member taking a turn to be Chairman for a single or series of meetings).

Controlling the meeting

Chairing a meeting requires a number of skills – perhaps akin to driving a team of horses. Without damping the enthusiasm and drive of individual members, their varying aims need to be drawn together and pushed in one general direction by someone in control. That someone is the Chairman and thus a number of qualities are required:

- leadership skills
- a strong personality
- vision
- communication skills
- enthusiasm
- the ability to delegate effectively
- the ability to control and direct
- setting and meeting the aims of the company (and of the Board)
- encouraging the Board to concentrate on the business in hand
- ensuring decisions are arrived at (and recorded), and
- motivating members.

In addition, a prime task is to ensure the effectiveness of meetings and their members. It may be necessary to issue a guide on the way members are expected to prepare for and even submit items for decision at the Board (see DATA SUBMISSION CONTROL).

The position of the Chairman is pivotal in terms of the effectiveness of the meeting and its approach to and determination of its work, and how such work and the members are manipulated and guided. Essentially, the meeting itself will normally reflect far more the character, drive and inspiration of the Chairman than any other factor or member. If this is not so then it is likely that the meeting is being dominated by someone other than the Chairman.

The Chairman's duties are:

a) to take responsibility for pushing the meeting itself to consider all its business (but equally only its business) and to attain its aims;

b) to know what is trying to be achieved from each item of business and from the entire meeting;

c) to ensure that not only is each item on the agenda dealt with comprehensively, but also that all members are heard on the subject, which may mean actively inviting members to contribute, rather than passively waiting for them to do so;

d) to bring the meeting back to the business in hand should it stray from such considerations;

e) to close down members' arguments or contentions where these threaten to swamp consideration of the subject matter and are not progressing the discussion. This is particularly relevant if the meeting is (or individual items are) subject to a time limit. The problem is that often the value of such member's contribution is in inverse proportion to the amount of time they spend propounding it. Moving the meeting on can then take a great deal of tact;

f) to ensure the decisions arrived at are recorded and promulgated and subsequent meetings are arranged only when business requires;

g) to lead the discussion and the meeting itself. A Chairman is a leader and an effective leader is someone who makes things happen and achieves results through people. The required work of the Chairman is thus to seek to make things happen through the members.

Despite the position of being 'first among equals' the meeting sits firmly in the control of the Chairman; after all the Chairman is usually the highest power within the organisation and very often, what he prefers becomes policy or practice. This gives the Chairman a great deal of power which must be used carefully and with discretion but can, of course, also be used less responsibly to attain personal aims.

The Chairman must know the purpose of the meeting, and by virtue of his position must endorse that purpose, so will wish to see the items of business considered by the meeting moved towards the attainment of the purposes. If he becomes aware of any possibility of this aim being frustrated, he may feel it to be his responsibility to try to 'take out' or 'neutralise' the opposition (see OUTFLANKING THE OPPOSITION and HOSTILITY). Since this may be difficult in the meeting itself, as it will gain attention and the opposition might gain support, it may be best for him to take the initiative in advance of the meeting.

Checklist

Chairmen should:
1. Seek to involve everyone.
2. Use open questions to generate information and involvement (even if they already know the answer).
3. Seek eye contact with all members.
4. Play to members' strengths and attempt to compensate for their weaknesses.
5. Insist that only one person speaks at a time and preferably in response to the Chairman's prompt.
6. Constantly try to summarise arguments and points to reach a consensus.
7. Avoid destructive criticism – temper criticism with positive comments.
8. Control without eliminating humour,
9. If discussion becomes heated, suggest a short break, possibly speaking to antagonists during this adjournment and attempting if not a reconciliation of views, some compromise.
10. Set a rough time limit for each item/the meeting and keep to it.
11. Listen carefully to what is said and watch body language to try to gauge what is not being said. There is a great deal of research on body language and it had been calculated that as much as 93 per cent of the 'message' in a face-to-face encounter is conveyed by body language and only 7 per cent by the words used. Caution is needed, however, in trying to reach conclusions from body language as attitudes, posture, etc. can give misleading information.

Chairmen should not:
1. Interrupt speakers unless they are waffling or straying from the point (or being abusive, etc.),
2. Prevent members from speaking. If the member has a right to be at

the meeting, he has a right to be heard (subject to the courtesies set out above).

3. Become personal – the subject matter should be the items on the Agenda not the members themselves.

4. Allow the discussion to meander without purpose – the aim must be to reach a decision (even if it has to be that the matter must be postponed pending further discussion, etc.).

Motivating the members

In fact, this may not be difficult since if people can identify with a successful effort, most tend to co-operate and work more effectively (and at Board level, if members cannot do this, there must be a question over their appointment and retention). If those involved have something of which they can be proud, and know that their contribution is important to the meeting and the organisation, they should have a commitment to a far higher level than would otherwise the case. In any event, commitment to a process of involvement tends to create an environment in which individuals work willingly.

Within an established meeting consensus may often be achieved, although there may be instances when conflict will surface. Indeed, it is arguable that a certain amount of constructive conflict can generate ideas and move the meeting towards its aims. If destructive conflict arises, the Chairman needs to be able either to remove it or direct it positively.

Thus the task of the Chairman is to combine 'progress chasing' with motivating and leading, and this triple role should always be recognised. In the latter endeavour the Chairman should ensure the best of each member is brought out within the meeting. It can be easy for a dominant person to take over the meeting and for less dominant members to be overshadowed to such an extent that they make little or no contribution. If this occurs, the Chairman's responsibility is to encourage the quieter members to make a contribution, even, if necessary, silencing others in order for them to do so. In this the Chairman will need to adopt the following guidelines:

a) Ensure everyone knows why they are present. In this the Chairman may need to restate the meeting's objectives. He may also state the time within which he would like to see the business conducted (on an overall and/or individual item basis). Such strictures must be promoted positively, the aim being to complete the business properly, recognising that time is scarce and valuable.

b) Treat every member as an individual with rights to make the points he or she wishes. This may require the Chairman actually inviting a contribution by name from the more reticent members.

c) Encourage every member to identify with the body as a whole and to relate to every other member. This will take time and, with some members, can be difficult.

d) Encourage a sense of pride in the meeting and its achievements. Without being excessive, the Chairman should praise achievements whether these be joint or individual. As a nation we in the UK tend to criticise too much and praise too little, even though praise (which costs nothing) can be the most powerful motivator and incentive. It is also helpful when trying to manage a meeting, since this 'feel good' effect can stifle or neutralise what could otherwise be objections.

e) Ensure all members are treated fairly and given a chance both to explain their views and attitudes and to argue their case. This in turn requires the opposition to have a chance to do the same. If members see that each is allowed his own turn to put forward arguments, the temptation to filibuster or use other means by which the arguments of others are not heard should be reduced.

f) Ensure members feel that business which they feel is important does get discussed. This may be difficult in the early life of a meeting and the Chairman needs to be tactful in accepting or rejecting business requested by members. If it is entirely germane to the business in hand, it may be worth considering, even if that in turn means the meeting overruns its allotted time span. If it is not appropriate, a tactful suggestion (for example, 'Perhaps we could have an initial chat about that after the meeting') might solve the problem without demotivating the member.

Briefing

Although in most cases a Chairman may be his own best counsel, at times it may be helpful for the Chairman to be given assistance – often the SECRETARY being a confidant, possible advising on any undercurrents he has noted from members, etc. In addition, the first time the Chairman needs to chair a more formal meeting than the average Board Meeting usually is (for example, the Annual General Meeting), the switch from the relative informality of a Board Meeting to the more formal requirements of a higher profile 'external' meeting can be somewhat daunting. Hence having a guide can assist – if only to ensure that the exact wording of the resolutions is adhered to. (See BRIEFING THE CHAIRMAN.)

Silencing opposition

In HOSTILITY a number of suggestions are made regarding the treatment of hostile meeting members or delegates – including the concept of splitting blocs of opposition. As well as physically separating opponents, the Chairman has power to downgrade their contribution by:

- 'not seeing' that they wish to make a contribution and thus not inviting their input;
- 'cutting across' their contribution should they stray for one moment from the core of the subject;
- applying debating devices (such as 'kangaroo' or 'closure' motions, which restrict comments to a short period).

Should the situation develop where a project thought to be essential for the business is likely to fail, due to the activities of the opposition, despite all the steps taken to negate their impact, the Chairman may need to act swiftly to ensure its survival, if not at the current meeting, then at an adjournment or subsequent meeting. In such a situation, the Chairman, anticipating the outvoting and defeat may need either to withdraw the item, to propose that it 'be left on the table', that is held over until the following meeting, or to adjourn the meeting itself. His powers to perform any or all of these acts will depend on the terms of reference of the meeting and it is essential that he is aware of the terms of reference and delineation of such powers.

Protecting the meeting

Once meeting members have been operating together as an entity for some time they will often coalesce as a team. Whilst their composition remains constant this rapport can be valuable and it may be possible to speed and improve decision-making. The inclusion of outsiders in the meeting may then detract from these advantages and thus the Chairman needs to consider and control their attendance carefully.

In addition, if the number of participants is swollen by those who either have no purpose being there or whose contribution is minimal or useless, then effectiveness will also be impaired – not least by those who consider themselves as effective members resenting the lack of effectiveness of such colleagues. Restricting membership to 'essential members only' may need to be qualified with some 'review of business meetings' where the progress of several disciplines is to be considered. Even in this scenario, however, attendance of people not involved in every item should be restricted so that they 'visit' the meeting only when required. Obviously, this may be difficult to monitor, particularly if, having given their report and left the meeting, a further matter arises affecting their area of responsibility. However, this is a situation where the Chairman needs to coach members to prepare for reports from such 'visiting executives' and to try to deal with all matters affecting them during their fleeting 'report only' visits. Alternatively, it may be possible to group disciplines under the control of permanent members of the meeting, and for them to each hold a separate review meeting outside the main meeting to allow meeting non-members the opportunity of reporting in full there. The meeting members can then simply report in outline or on an 'exception basis'. This should mean that the meeting non-member (that is, the person with 'hands on' responsibility for the discipline) may be required to attend the main meeting only on an exception basis.

Gaining the sense of the meeting

In most meetings, decisions reflect the collective responsibility concept and the Chairman should summarise the arguments before taking the 'sense' or decision of the meeting. Usually each person entitled to be present has a right to be heard on each subject and this will usually be the case in most other meetings, as any alternative negates the purpose of the member's attendance. Whilst with a committee of long standing the Chairman may be able to gain the sense of the meeting by means of a fairly informal question such as 'anyone anything else to say?', with a newer committee or meeting, a more structured approach may be necessary. To generate an individual contribution the Chairman might wish to address a member by name: 'Jean, I think you wished to contribute to this discussion but I don't recall hearing from you, do you have anything to add?' Even if Jean has nothing to add, she may well say a few words and will feel flattered that her contribution has been sought. If there has been some dissent or argument, the Chairman might wish to try to gather the threads together by addressing the leaders of disputing factions with the words 'Jo, are you sure you have now put all the facts to the meeting?' or 'Bill, have you had enough time to put your case?' Assuming both do contribute they will normally try to gain support from any waverers by summarising their most salient points. From their comments the Chairman can check that he has all the facts needed to provide an overall summary. Using this approach it should be difficult for anyone to complain of unfair treatment.

Perception

Essentially, chairing comes down to having a good perception or understanding of people. This is a skill which is easy to describe and sadly not so easy to achieve, still less apply. Yet in attempting to move colleagues or meeting members to a predetermined outcome or desired result, it is essential that their views and opinions, prejudices and preferences, attitudes and previous reactions are all taken into account to guide one to tactics likely to gain their support. If this approach sounds as though it has political overtones, that is hardly surprising, after all politics has been defined as the art of the possible, and what is being suggested is that those that have determined a particular outcome then need to consider how to move others to their way of thinking.

An old saying goes: 'The reason we have one mouth and two ears is so that we can listen twice as much as we talk.' Sadly, in practice this tends to be the exception, and can be aggravated by the passive state of hearing being mistaken for the active state of actually listening to what a person is saying. Indeed, active listening requires us to consider not just what a person says, but also what they do *not* say, and what can be inferred from body language, attitudes and actions. After all, a person is quite capable of a multiple response to a given situation. He may well reply to the same question in totally different terms to his boss, his colleagues, his subordinate and his partner, whilst all the time keeping his real feelings strictly to himself! Perception requires us to try to comprehend and understand those true feelings. Ignoring such feelings may ultimately provide us with a problem in achieving a determined outcome.

Avoiding adverse reactions

The Chairman will achieve his purpose by gaining the appropriate decisions to items of business. At times, however, he may find that such a decision is not forthcoming. This may result from an item of business being sprung on a committee, or where an alliance of members with majority voting power unexpectedly raises such an item safe in the knowledge that its success is assured, both from the fact that support has already been canvassed and that opposition will be unprepared and so unable to combat it effectively. The ambush is effective where support is assured, but less so where the case needs to be argued, particularly if this is necessary to win over support. In these circumstances negotiations, or at least exploration of the case, in advance of the meeting may be advisable. Few people like losing out or ending up on the wrong side, particularly in a semi-public forum such as a meeting, and such a public defeat may be avoided by broaching the subject with colleagues in advance, gaining their reactions and either toning down or altering aspects of the suggestion or, if there seems to be little support or total animosity, dropping the idea altogether.

Such a strategy has a number of advantages:

- It grants the member the reputation of being a good team player. Reputation and respect can help win arguments in meetings and dealing with a possibly controversial matter outside the meeting, particularly if it concerns or is raised with the Chairman, may well earn the instigator some prestige for future use, even though the actual subject matter gains no support on the present occasion.
- It avoids embarrassing the person with whom it is raised as it could

were it to be raised in open meeting, which may give the instigator a slight edge in other circumstances. The position of that person, particularly if he is the Chairman, is thus protected. He can explain opposition or reaction in private, and possibly even in confidence, to the instigator, without the public pressure of the meeting.

- It enables the instigator to gain some measure of the depth of feeling likely to be encountered were the matter to be raised in meeting. If the reaction is very hostile he can back off immediately, excusing himself with some reference to its being an idle thought or even an idea that someone else had mentioned to him!
- The concept itself is brought into the open. Whilst it may not gain support this time around, repeated references to the idea may ultimately win over those formerly antagonistic to it, particularly if later events are used to illustrate its advisability.

Crisis communication

Introduction

Increasingly, the activities of organisations – particularly wealth-creating organisations – are of considerable interest to the media. Even though in most cases the interest arises purely from a desire to fill column inches or air time, this interest must be recognised and arrangements made to provide information on a regular written basis and/or by telephone or face-to-face discussions or meetings. The organisation needs to plan for such interest, to have a procedure for dealing with the media, particularly when there is a crisis, and to coach spokesmen to brief media representatives.

Policy

The adoption of a policy for dealing with the media is essential and the policy set out in MEDIA AND PUBLIC RELATIONS could be utilised as a base. It should assist when there is a crisis, if relationships are built up during normal times. Given the media's predilection for bad news stories this may be easier said than done. If, however, briefing the media on the more mundane aspects of company performance may not create much interest, dealing with such interest in the aftermath of a calamity or disaster, poses considerable problems capable of being tackled effectively only if there has been attention to contingency planning. Contingency planning involves anticipating the disaster and making plans for dealing with predicted or anticipated effects. The advantage of 'planning for disaster' is that lengthy and calm thought can be given to alternative tactics and reactions, without the considerable time pressure for reaction that the incidence of disaster can cause. In addition, consideration of alternative actions in the event of disaster, may suggest beneficial changes in current operations. Obviously, if it is to be of value such planning must be both comprehensive and regularly updated and one aspect needs to address the interest of the media and how it should be handled.

Checklist

1. Initial contact will usually be by telephone. A person should be nominated, possibly the Company Secretary, though there should always be one or two back-up personnel to handle initial queries if the spokesperson is not available. Other employees should be instructed to refer any approaches to the spokesperson.
2. Keep calm and listen to what the inquirer is asking.
3. Make notes of, or tape, the call content, time, the caller's name, position and media represented, the caller's telephone number and location.
4. Do *not* respond to questions, comments, observations – simply make notes as set out in 3. above and state that by a (stated) time someone will respond either in a press release or by telephone, and so on.
5. Do *not* be flustered by indications of deadlines, insistence on immediate response, outrageous accusations or innuendo.
6. By the time promised, not less than an hour, ensure someone does ring the caller back with comments.
7. Keep responses, press statements, and so on, short. Embroidery can both offset the punch effect and provide other 'angles' from which the reporter can come back at the author.
8. Provide a contact name/number.
9. Should such contact be used then the above guidelines should be applied. If necessary the spokesperson should ring back after time for thought.
10. If a media information release is to be used, these need to be drafted carefully so that:
    a) the essential features of the news to be reported is contained in the first paragraph;
    b) the news must be of substance and presented concisely and clearly;
    c) it provides quotable quotes from named authorities; and
    d) it specifies a realistic release date and gives an in-house contact and telephone number.

Interviews

The spokesperson needs considerable personal knowledge of the organisation. This can be augmented by detailed input from time to time by those personally responsible. However such background, whilst essential, is not sufficient. Excellent Chairmen (the normal spokesmen for corporate matters) do not necessarily make excellent spokesmen when other issues are under review and training for such circumstances is essential. The person must be able to:

- keep calm under pressure;
- keep very calm in the face of what might even be insulting questions (deliberately phrased that way to try to make the target lose their temper);
- think swiftly;
- appreciate that some answers may be double-edged (i.e. that either of two responses may be self-critical) and to try to avoid this effect, and to show their knowledge is sound.

The items in the following checklist should be addressed:

Checklist: Spokesperson interview briefing

1. Before agreeing to the interview discover as much as possible about the circumstances (name of interviewer, programme, general purpose, scope of enquiry, whether live or recorded, scope for restricting/controlling questions, length of item to be used and likely use date, etc.).
2. As comprehensive and complete a brief as possible must be prepared on the subject matter and supporting items – organisation data, performance, products, problems, plans, etc.
3. If the topic is likely to be controversial or embarrassing to the person or organisation, appropriate responses and statements should be prepared (trying to limit the 'damage' that could be caused) and/or news which mitigates the effect should be developed.
4. The spokesperson needs to have total control of the brief, of all facts and of prepared responses, to be able to speak knowledgeably concerning the subject matter. Any hesitation, lack of confidence or inadequate knowledge will be communicated to the listener or viewer and can create doubt and/or undermine veracity. In this respect it may be better to admit 'I don't know' rather than trying to 'flannel' through an answer. At least saying 'I don't know' (although it should only be used once or twice in any one interview) does have the ring of truth about it and can indicate – and may win some praise for – honesty and straightforwardness.
5. Three or four simple messages, or arguments that the organisation wishes to promote, must be developed, possibly with 'changes of direction' sentences, so that if the interviewer leads off in one direction, the spokesperson may be able to direct it to

the organisation's preferred messages. This approach needs to be controlled since a constant refusal to answer the actual questions put may lead to a more inquisitive or confrontational interview.

6. There should be no assumption that the interviewer will not have full knowledge of all the facts. It is better to assume that everything is known and then prepare answers accordingly.

7. The spokesperson must be ready for the 'off the cuff' and unrehearsed question deliberately introduced and designed to catch him/her unawares leading to the making of an unprepared or unwise comment or answer.

8. Above all the spokesperson must be able to keep calm under pressure and/or goading, to be able to think quickly and laterally in order to fend off or turn aggression and criticism, to retain control, and never to lose their temper.

Case study: *Lose your temper – lose the argument*

During one of the periodical examinations of top people's pay the Chairman of one of the privatised utilities was being interviewed on television. His salary had recently been increased substantially and the interviewer wanted an explanation. Instead of explaining the impact of market forces on salaries, the increased productivity achieved and liabilities accepted, and other quantifiable achievements, the Chairman lost his temper on camera. The sight was unedifying and displayed a lack of preparedness for the questions which reflected badly not only on the Chairman but also on his staff, who should have briefed him.

---

9. The spokesperson must recognise that most live media interviews last a minute or less and thus it may be possible only to put across two or three authoritative comments. They need to be calm, alert and interested and serious – a spokesperson should never try to be humorous, flustered or flippant. To a large extent, particularly on television, the manner in which a message is delivered can be more effective than the content.

10. They should take time to think about the questions – asking for them to be repeated if necessary – but not too long.

11. False statements should not be allowed to pass unchecked – the record should be corrected, tactfully but firmly.

12. Be positive not defensive. It may be better to own up to a bad performance or event with a promise to improve or rectify, rather than trying to defend an untenable position. The latter alternative will normally display the organisation in a poor light regardless of the circumstances – the impression will be 'they have learned nothing from the mistake, so nothing will change'. This is particularly important when there has been loss, injury or death. In such instances it is essential that genuine sympathy is expressed and that there is an indication that steps are being taken to try to ensure there is no repetition.

Preparation

The key to being able to deal with the crisis positively is preparation and the ability to view the problem and the situation from the point of view of those involved and those who will hear the news cold (i.e. who are not personally involved).

Case studies: *Doasyouwouldbedoneby*

Making employees redundant can have considerable repercussions unless it is planned for and dealt with tactfully.

1. When Maynards closed their Bristol warehouse, the details of the economic difficulties facing the division of which it was part, as well as the redundancy payments of all the employees affected were calculated individually and details of outplacement services were formulated. Two main Board directors travelled down the previous night and in the morning interviewed all the staff, first *en masse* and then individually (when the figures were made available). Every meeting went smoothly, with several employees (most of whom had a considerable amount of service with the company) actually thanking the directors for 'the way it had been done'.

2. Similarly when Stag Furniture Holdings realised there was overcapacity in the industry and decided they would need to close a factory (coincidentally also near Bristol), there was

---

considerable consultation with unions, employees, local press and all other involved parties. The process went smoothly – there was no industrial action and production carried on smoothly. The consultations were handled by the Managing Director, whilst the Chairman (at the Head Office in Nottingham) was available to talk to the media.

The point about both events was that unions and employees (as well as third parties) were aware that the decisions were appropriate and right for the organisation even if not for them. People are quite capable of dealing positively with bad news provided:

a)   they are treated as responsible human beings;
b)   it is obvious their views have been taken into account (which is not a legal requirement); and
c)   the bad news is not attempted to be concealed by the use of jargon (one definition of which is 'the meaningless babble of an infant').

Customer care

Introduction

Aided by an increasing range of protective legislation and a greater preparedness to complain and protest at what they perceive to be poor or inadequate service or quality, the twenty-first century is likely to see the balance of the terms of trade moving far more in favour of the consumer. Either voiced directly with the organisation (backed with a threat real or imagined to use the power of the media to provide adverse publicity if suitable recompense is not made available) or to local Trading Standards Officers or the Office of Fair Trading (to whom 'unfair contract terms' can be reported) an increasing number of customers are prepared to make their views known. Trying to please the existing, attract the prospective and avoid dissatisfying customers should be a high priority – indeed, it is difficult to think of a higher aim for the Board. Not only may disenchanted customers' purchasing power be lost, which may cause other custom to be lost, but also it is five times as expensive to attract a new customer than it is to retain an existing customer. Only if customers are pleased and retained does the Board properly exercise its stewardship of the shareholders' assets – a truism often overlooked.

The ostrich approach

Whilst it appears that some, even high-profile organisations are prepared to shrug off criticism or stubbornly defend what appear to be indefensible positions thus creating disenchanted customers (and thereby creating a need to invest simply to replace the lost sale), organisations which value their reputation, need to try to ensure that they 'keep the customer satisfied'. In the UK and Europe there was a considerable shrinking of demand as a result of the worldwide recession of the early 1990s. In many, particularly more traditional, businesses the level of trade will not regain its former level until around 2005. For such businesses – and others – simply trying to retain their existing customer base may be a major survival factor. The loyalty of customers will only be retained if they are satisfied – in many instances there is usually another supplier (and sometimes more than one) well able to take the dissatisfied customers' business. Unfortunately, the organisation may only be aware of the true reaction of a tiny proportion of its customers before it is too late. The US White House Office of Consumer Affairs found in research for its Technical Assistance and Research Programme that businesses do not hear from 96 per cent of their dissatisfied customers – and that for every complaint that is received there are a further 26 silent customers of whom six have serious problems. Presumably most of this silent majority votes with their feet and/or purse in a different direction.

Reputation

Handled well, customer complaints can enhance the reputation of the organisation – handled badly, the reputation of the organisation can be severely damaged. Tony Palmer, chief executive of construction giant, Taylor Woodrow, states that a good corporate image can make customers between 1 per cent and 5 per cent more willing to buy – often enough to tip the balance in a company's favour. Taylor Woodrow trained its 8,500 staff to enhance the company's image by doing and saying the right thing: 'in interfacing with customers, we need all our staff to understand public relations,' the company maintains. For 'understanding public relations' we could substitute 'know how to foster positive customer communication in all instances'. It might be beneficial to link the activities of the Customer Care and those responsible for MEDIA INTERFACING. Experience suggests that normally the two are remote despite the former being one of the most important foundations of the latter. A dissatisfied customer is likely to tell a great number of others of the poor service or unsatisfactory treatment he has received: Syd Pennington, Managing Director of Virgin Atlantic suggests that a dissatisfied customer will tell around 17 others of his bad treatment. Those who know their way around may find other outlets – consumer protection programmes on both radio and television, national press articles, and so on – which could increase this number dramatically. Poisoning customer demand in this way is easy, particularly as some customers and reporters will not resist the temptation to exaggerate to 'make the case' (or simply, and perhaps understandably, to make a better story!). In increasingly competitive times this could cost the organisation dearly – every lost customer needs to be replaced simply to maintain the status quo. Such an effort (even though it costs five times as much as retaining the existing customer) is purely protective – it fails completely to drive the company forward.

Senior accountability

Very often what virtually amounts to an invitation to a dissatisfied customer to 'poison the waters' is a result of a defensive or unthinking attitude at a fairly low level in an organisation. This is not the fault of the employee. To ensure that customer communication is always positive and follows management's commitment to this ideal, all employees who interface with customers must be trained to provide a positive approach – to see the complaint through the eyes of the customer who can choose to buy or not, rather than the organisation which must sell to survive. It might assist in commencing such training if the fact that an organisation can only survive if it satisfies and keeps satisfying its customers – and more of them – is promoted as the initial and prime contention. Obviously, if enough customers are dissatisfied, there can be no employment but despite this truism adverse reactions to customer queries are widespread in the UK – a phenomenon somewhat at variance with experience on the Continent and in the US. This is not to imply that every customer is always right – sometimes complaints are unjustified and unreasonable, and need to be resisted. Very often, however, observations are denied in a totally unreasonable way and the potential effect on the reputation of the business and the retention of other customers is totally overlooked.

Unwise delegation

The main problem is that Boards generally delegate customer care well down the line and, whilst they may require statistics on 'complaints', etc., they receive all such information secondhand. If there is no direct Board level commitment – which means 'hands-on' director involvement in the area of customer care – the wrong message (e.g. 'they're not really worried upstairs, so it's not really important – get rid of that complaint and get on with the next one') is being understood by those interfacing directly with the customer. Many Boards adopt the hackneyed phrase 'the customer must come first' without committing themselves to interfacing directly with the customer to check whether this aspiration is borne out by the customers' experience. Very often the reality is far removed from the rhetoric. Yet keeping the customer satisfied is an absolutely crucial area of the Board's responsibilities. Unless the customers and more of them are kept satisfied the Board will swiftly have no business.

Case study:	*Arrogance can be costly*
	Writing in the *Financial Times*, a former BA customer complained at British Airways arrogant attitude to their economy class passengers and stated that because of it he had experimented with an alternative airline. He received what he regarded as better service and remained with them for 14 years – spending in excess of $150,000. All this was turnover lost to BA.

Undeterred BA has recently further alienated such customers by extending the number of and space for its 'executive rate' customers, arguing that the Pareto law applies. Vifredo Pareto was a Paris-born Italian economist who is credited with developing the rule: '80 per cent of profit is derived from 20 per cent of customers'. However, removing the 80 per cent of customers from whom only 20 per cent of profits is derived means that the costs formerly shared by the whole have now to be shared by the few – making some of them in turn less profitable than the norm. In addition, others are always prepared to accommodate 'lost customers', which will help grow their businesses and pose a long-term potential threat. (In fact Pareto maintained that despite all attempts to change it, income distribution remains constant!)

As a further dimension to the danger of slimming the product appeal, much business travel is for meetings. It is estimated that European companies spend around £100 billion each year on travel and associated costs. Whilst there are currently severe disadvantages with VIRTUAL MEETINGS, no doubt their use will grow – and the demand for business travel could diminish substantially.

Consultants Price Waterhouse surveyed the top 200 UK companies and found that under 10 per cent analysed how many customers they lose every year even though they estimated that customer defection loses British industry around £100 *billion* each year – about the same amount that is spent on marketing, sales and distribution (at least in part trying to attract new customers!). The company that loses 10 per cent of its customers each year without replacing them will be out of business in under five years – and many companies would go under in a far shorter period. Such a scenario would take some explanation to the shareholders. Indeed, it is not impossible to imagine a situation where shareholders could take action against a Board that failed to give customer care and the protection of the customer base their required and critical priority.

DARN

In ONE STOP Customer Care the mnemonic DARN is used to symbolise the process needed. The process of darning in needlework is to repair and make as new, and this is the underlying message of the mnemonic in the context of handling customer queries and complaints. Where customers have problems, a break has occurred in the 'fabric' of the relationship between supplier and purchaser. DARN stands for Discovery, Apology, Rectification and Novation – four stages of the process by which the 'fabric' of damaged sales can be repaired.

Checklist

1. By actively listening, avoiding defensive justification and asking open questions the person fielding the complaint should record the facts so that the organisation can (D for) Discover and identify the problem experienced by the customer. Not only should openness, a willingness to listen and checking all the facts be undertaken, but the customer needs to see that they their complaint is being taken seriously. This process can be extended to ask the customer, having gained such details, what is their desired result is – what is it that they want? In this way the conversation can be converted from a negative 'Let's record your complaint' to a positive 'What can we do about this?' discussion which restores the choice the customer had before he bought the product.

2. If the organisation is at fault (and even if it is not or the responsibility of fault is unclear) this should generate an early A for Apology. Apologising can draw the sting from most such complaints. Faced with intransigence or negative defence of a position, it is all too easy for disappointed customers to lose their temper and become more demanding. But when the other party is apologising many people warm to them and lose their anger – rather than their temper. It can be difficult to maintain anger or annoyance when the other party seems genuinely sorry and is, apparently, trying to rectify the matter.

3. R for Rectification. Since the supplier is at fault (and even if it is not since it may be counter-productive to dispute if the value of possible recompense is small) it should seek to make amends. Here, using the telephone to 'do a deal' with the complainant can be very useful since any offer need not be committed to paper and thus no evidence will exist for use as a precedent. This echoes the point made under D for Discovery. Finding out what it is the customer wants (i.e. restoring choice) turns the conversation into positive mode.

4. Finally, the darning process ends with N for Novation which is concerned with any changes that the organisation may need to make to the product, process, system, administration or promotional material which has been shown to be faulty. It may be that an analysis of complaints can aid the development of whatever it is that is at fault.

Data submission control

Introduction

When setting up a new meeting or revising the operation of an existing one, or when there has been some abuse of the submission of documentation of data for consideration at a meeting, it may be helpful and/or necessary to issue guidelines regarding the expectations of the meeting members in regard to the receipt of data on which they need to make decisions at their meetings. Whilst inevitably circumstances will sometimes require that these are ignored, generally such guidelines should be adhered to.

Requiring members to comply with controls regarding the submission of data and reports should remove any emotive reactions when the Chairman refuses to allow the meeting to consider a late submitted report since it will be rejected 'in accordance with standing instructions' not on a current whim. It is also a sound way of creating good habits.

Checklist

Requirements to be issued to all meeting members and those submitting information to be considered at the meeting.

A. Timetable
1. A timetable for the use of all required to attend, submit data to, and draw information from the meeting will be prepared on a rolling six-month basis and issued by the meeting convener.
2. Other than in the most exceptional instances, the timing of meetings will not be changed and any member unable to attend must let the meeting convener know as soon as possible.
3. An agenda with supporting data should always be issued at least [7] working days prior to a meeting.

B. Data required
1. As a matter of routine all information and reports should be made available to the meeting convenor at least [8] working days before the meeting.

2. All data should be submitted with the stated number of copies required.

Notes

a) The stated number could be the number of persons entitled to receive the agenda plus any required to be sent out for information, plus spares in the proportion of one for each five persons on the distribution list.

b) Where it is usual for a number of documents to accompany the agenda, colour coding such documentation could be considered.

---

3. If data are not available to meet the submission deadline an indication of the availability date must be given, the Chairman must be informed and a note of the expected date of receipt/issue entered on the Agenda.

Note

Those submitting data late must make every effort to convey it direct to the meeting members prior to the meeting with the required number of spares to the meeting convener. Asking for data to be allowed to be tabled at the meeting, particularly if it consists of detailed, involved or lengthy reports may result in the item being 'left on the table' for consideration at a later meeting.

---

4. Documentation will be presented in agenda order.

C. Presentation
1. Every item prepared for the [Board/committee] will be required to have a standard covering sheet (see F below).
2. Subsequent sheets may be presented in the format most suitable for the subject matter.
3. The utmost brevity, commensurate with the subject matter, should be employed. Commentary should be avoided and facts and suppositions, and opposing data, suitably differentiated must be presented clearly.
4, Source(s) of data should be referenced, and a summary used, rather than including such data as part of the submission.
5. The conclusions and recommendations, as required to be set out on the covering page (see below), must be clearly evidenced within the report.

6. Plain English should be used and jargon avoided. Where jargon is essential, a glossary accurately defining the terms used should be included.

D. Supporting commentary

1. At the meeting, the report's originator or person responsible for the subject matter should be prepared to speak to the report, to answer questions from other members and generally to assist the meeting to come to a suitable decision regarding its content.
2. Should the meeting require amplifying documentation this must be provided in the same format as that used in the original report and submitted for the next following meeting.
3. Proposers should endeavour to speak only once to support or promote the subject matter and should therefore cover all salient facts in their short presentation.

Note

This will entail marshalling all facts, data, comments, and so on, balancing brevity against comprehensiveness, highlighting only the most important aspects and avoiding repetition, other than when necessary as a result of other members' questions.

---

4. Other meeting members should similarly endeavour to speak only once, putting forward their objections or comments in the same manner as set out in D3 above.
5. After such proposal and counter-comments, if the subject is of such import the Chairman may wish to encourage a short general discussion on the subject, otherwise the next move will be to summarise the content and take the sense of the meeting.

E. Decisions

Decisions will be communicated by the meeting convener and/or the sponsoring member. If approved or referred back for reconsideration the decision will be supported by a copy of the minutes dealing with the subject which will include any conditions, timing, capital expenditure, and so on.

F. Covering sheet

Organisation name

Report title .... Date of report ....

Author/sponsoring dept ....

Date to be considered by meeting ....

Subject matter ....

....

Recommendations 1 ....

2 ....

3 ....

Résumé of facts/contentions supporting recommendations ....

....

....

....

Résumé of facts/contentions contesting recommendations ....

....

....

....

Implications for organisation if not proceeded with ....

....

....

Capital expenditure implications ....

....

....

Skill/personnel implications ....

....

Timing required ....

Outline required first page of all Board/committee reports

Note

Formal rules of debate may be applied in certain circumstances and/ or organisations. The following is a résumé:

1. In order for business to proceed it will be expected that business will receive support from at least one other member of the meeting who will normally second the proposal.
2. If no support is forthcoming, then the Chairman will have authority

to rule that no further discussion ensues and the proposed item will fail.

3. The proposer of an item of business, having put the business to the meeting, will have a right of reply to points raised against it by other members.

4. Normally each member, other than the proposer, will be able to speak on each item of business once only.

5. Once business has been put to the meeting, other than with the consent of the meeting, it cannot be withdrawn.

Disciplinary interviews

Introduction

In all employing organisations, from time to time there will be a need to conduct a disciplinary interview. Although many will regard such interviews as an essentially private matter between manager and employee, in some cases it is possible for there ultimately to be a public dimension. The record and outcome of an interview handled badly (that is, not in accordance with an employer's procedure and/or legal requirements) could one day be inspected by an Employment Tribunal and even by the national media (whose interest in Tribunal cases continues to grow). There is thus a potential for considerable damage being caused to the reputation of the employing organisation if such events are poorly handled. Indeed, should an organisation gain a reputation for being a poor employer not only could morale suffer (which itself could lead to further disciplinary problems, increased absenteeism and petty pilfering, etc.) and increased labour turnover, but also difficulty could well be experienced in attracting new applicants.

Purpose

There are two main reasons for disciplinary interviews being necessary – to state that an employee is not performing or behaving in the desired fashion and to demonstrate how this can be rectified and to prepare a case that could ultimately lead to dismissal. Unfortunately, some employers tend to regard such interviews as solely of the latter variety. In 1996 Dr Derek Rollinson canvassed the opinions of over 100 employees who had been subject to their employers' disciplinary processes. Many felt that their cases had been dealt with in an unfair way. Only 24 per cent stated that they now observed the rules they had been disciplined for breaking, whilst a further 24 per cent stated that they obeyed the rules grudgingly. The employees who had changed their habits to avoid breaching the rules, stated that their managers had taken a persuasive line, 'sometimes spending more than an hour getting the employee to understand that a rule had been breached'.

In most other cases the employees felt the managers had assumed guilt and were simply going through the motions. The hidden messages from these approaches are obvious – and can be easily understood by employees other than those disciplined.

Procedure

All such interviews should be conducted exactly in accordance with the procedure laid down by the employer. Thus the procedure itself needs to be clear and concise and be made available to all. In addition, those who need to apply it in practice need to be coached so that their actions, each in exact accordance with it, occur automatically as routine.

Ideally, a disciplinary procedure (and especially any appeal procedure) should be kept as short, and with as few options, as possible. The more complex a procedure is, the more likely it is that at some stage there may be an unintended deviation from it by either party. Should the employer deviate from the procedure they may be unable to defend their actions successfully in a tribunal.

An employee should always be offered the opportunity of being accompanied by a representative to act as a witness. There is no need for the witness to say anything, although it may be helpful if they make notes of what transpired.

Record

Notes (ideally a verbatim record) should be kept of the proceedings and it is helpful if the employee is given a copy and requested within a specified time (e.g. two working days) to confirm that the notes are a true record of what transpired. Should the employee challenge the record it should be corrected unless the chairman of the proceedings feels the challenge/alteration is unwarranted.

Note

The advantage of making a verbatim record of such interviews is that composing a record from notes may 'place into the mouth of the employee' words and sentiments which are not their own but are an interpretation (even a translation) of what they said. Should the employee later challenge the record, it may be difficult for the employer to convince third parties that the record was entirely accurate.

> **Case study:** *Translation causes doubt*
>
> In a tribunal case concerning a dismissal following a
> scuffle between two employees – both over 6 feet tall
> and one of whom weighed around 18 stone – the
> record of a disciplinary interview lasting two hours
> placed before the tribunal was just two pages long. It
> contained so-called quotes from the applicant (who
> had been dismissed despite there having been
> extreme provocation) including:
>
> 'He [the 18 stone employee] swore and squared up to
> me and I subtly pushed him away.'
>
> 'He had previously put his hands in my pockets to
> which I had to retaliate as I am sensitive.'
>
> 'I think the problem was that we emanated from
> different cultures.'
>
> The applicant was an immigrant and English was not
> his native tongue. He was a shy man who had
> difficulty reading and expressing himself. The tribunal
> found it difficult to imagine him using words such as
> 'subtly' (particularly in the context of being squared
> up to by someone of the other's size), 'sensitive' and
> 'emanated'. In turn, this raised severe doubts about
> the accuracy of the record.

With the availability of inexpensive tape-recording equipment it may be
advisable to tape-record interviews concerned with more serious alle-
gations. If this alternative is used, then it would be advisable to make two
machines available so that a copy is available for the employee immediately
at the conclusion of the proceedings (as is the case following police interviews). A typed transcript of every word can then be prepared and since
two copies exist it will be difficult for this record to be challenged. In
addition, not only should the words be recorded but so also can the tone
and inflexions which can alter the words themselves.

Decision

Once all witnesses have been heard and each side has been able to question
them, and an opportunity has been given to each side to make final sub-
missions (which in the employee's case might include a plea for leniency

should their previous record have been good), a decision will need to be made. It may be helpful to adjourn whilst the Chairman considers the evidence, makes a decision and, if necessary, considers what would be a suitable penalty. This has the advantage of demonstrating (or at least implying) that justice is being done. The decision should be recorded in writing, particularly if any penalty is involved, since this should minimise the possibility of dispute about the result.

Agreeing a course of action

Where the matter is one of CAPABILITY or where a final warning is not required it may be helpful not only to consider a sanction but, having made the decision, to attempt to agree with the employee a course of action that will avoid any repetition. If the employee is involved in and discusses the suggested actions with the employer, they should 'own' the conclusions reached and thus be more prepared to attempt to attain them. Conversely, it could be difficult for them subsequently to deny that they had agreed such a course of action. Any agreement should be evidenced in writing and form part of the disciplinary hearing record.

Appeal

As mentioned above, rules concerning appeals should be kept as brief and as clear as possible and very few restrictions should be applied. Indeed, there is an argument for providing internal advice regarding lodging an appeal to ensure fairness. Rejecting an application for appeal requires explanation and carries an automatic inference of unfairness. Allowing an appeal to be heard, even one of dubious merit, conveys the message that here is an employer determined to be fair. These hidden messages can convey very powerful inferences to those watching the transaction.

The hidden watchers

Although a disciplinary interview may be handled with discretion and a degree of confidentiality, inevitably in most instances details of the 'offence' and the decision will be rumoured and, since such decisions provide proof of the attitude of the employer, will be the subject of considerable interest. For this reason proceedings and decisions need to be:

- entirely in accordance with procedures;
- fair and reasoned and sustainable in terms of precedent;
- in keeping with the rules and regulations of the employer.

In addition the decisions – warnings, suspension, dismissal, etc. – need to be both fair and to be seen to be fair.

Guidance

It may be helpful to keep a central record of disciplinary meetings so that those managers needing to conduct such hearings can read first-hand accounts of previous instances and obtain an insight into the way the organisation wishes interviews to be conducted. Exercising control over and applying sanctions to employees is a right of every employer – but this right entails considerable responsibilities to ensure fairness and consistency. Getting it wrong can send a variety of messages to interested parties.

Employee communication

Introduction

The Confederation of British Industry is on record as stating that 'effective communication with employees will be one of the major issues facing [employers] management over the next decade'. The questions of how, what and when to communicate and/or inform needs to be determined at a policy-making level. A communication policy is a statement made and disseminated by an organisation through which it commits itself to the regular production and distribution of information and/or allows two-way transference of information (i.e. true communication). Inevitably, whilst some links with employees can be generated by the provision of information, there is a need for a range of meetings (some the subject of separate sections in this book) to generate proper two-way communication.

Communication is not information

Before considering the policy committing employers to employee communication, it is helpful to distinguish between the terms 'information' and 'communication', not least since they are often used as if they were synonyms, which is far from the case.

Despite communication being essential in all human life, let alone in economic endeavour, the word and the ensuing process is often misunderstood or confused. Nowhere is this more true than in an interface between just two participants, and if communication can be misunderstood between just two players the capacity for misunderstanding when there are a greater number of players is considerable.

Example

If A meets B and tells him that the production target for this week is 1,000 widgets, he may feel he is communicating with B. But this is not the case; he is merely giving B information. However, if A has a meeting with B, asks him what manpower he has available, whether

> there are adequate supplies of raw material and power, and whether there are any problems in attaining the week's production target, he has begun the communication process. If he then actively listens to, not passively 'hears' B's answers, which may themselves include problems requiring solution, and then A and B jointly decide a course of action, communication is in process and is helping attaining the joint ends of the participants' meeting.

True communication thus consists of a meeting of minds and a gaining of consensus (even if this is 'agreeing to differ'). It is essentially a two-way dialogue involving comprehension of both parties' viewpoints, concerns and priorities, which can only be achieved by an exchange of information and feedback. It is a dynamic, not a passive, process affecting all parties as is shown in Figure 3.

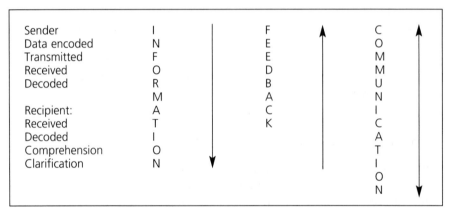

Figure 3 Information does not equate to communication
(from ONE STOP Communication)

Developing and promulgating a policy

With comprehension of the twin but different roles that can be played by these two vital components of ensuring employees work to attain the aims of the organisation, a policy demonstrating commitment to the principles needs to be developed.

Example

Policy

1. The [organisation] wishes to involve all personnel in its activities, to encourage their active participation in its progress including decision-making, and to benefit by their comments and ideas.
2. The [organisation] commits itself to the regular dissemination of information and to the encouragement of inter[organisation] and interpersonal communication meetings which are to encompass discussion of personal as well as organisational activities.
3. General aims. The [organisation] believes that people will give of their best when they are part of a fair-minded, well-disciplined and structured organisation which clearly sets out what is and is not expected of its employees and administers such rules impartially, without exception and in accordance with the rules of natural justice. The [organisation] encourages individual recognition of all employees by name by their immediate superiors, who are required to treat those for whom they are responsible as rational human beings. Those responsible for others should make themselves available to guide, help and coach as needed. Whilst the [organisation] will support managers and supervisors when they need to criticise and discipline their staff, it is stressed that praise should be given whenever it is warranted.
4. On appointment each employee will be given an information wallet containing:
   a) contract of employment
   b) employee handbook
   c) health, safety and fire precautions statements
   d) confidentiality and equal opportunity statements
   e) copy of latest employee report
   f) copy of latest newsletter (group)
   g) copy of any departmental/divisional/site publication

5. During employment employees will receive:
   a) annual/employee report (annually)
   b) interim results (annually)
   c) newsletter (quarterly/monthly/two weekly, etc.)
   d) local departmental/divisional/site newsletter or equivalent
6. Employees will also be expected to attend and contribute to:
   a) regular management organised briefing sessions, and
   b) ad hoc briefing session as required

and to:

c) representation at Works Council/joint consultative meetings
d) copies of Works Council/committee minutes
e) representation on safety/pensions/redundancy/other committee
f) copies of safety/other committee minutes

7. Ongoing commitment. Management are expected and encouraged to keep their employees informed of all activities and developments in an informal manner (either by informal one-to-one meetings or by team BRIEFING GROUPS), there being no substitute for such face-to-face communication.

8. Employees are encouraged to take a lively interest in the activities of the [organisation] and, should there be anything on which they have insufficient information or where they are unsure, should be encouraged to ask their immediate superior, and should they not receive an adequate answer, to pursue their query through the grievance procedure set out in the employee handbook.

9. Feedback (by both formal and informal means) will be sought from all employees on aspects of this policy.

10. Working unit briefing meetings will be held regularly throughout the [organisation]. These will be informal discussion opportunities at which everyone in the team is expected to participate. Questions asked during such sessions should either be answered (if known) there and then, or guidance sought and an answer provided by or at the next following briefing meeting.

11. Through the APPRAISAL procedure, managers and employees are required to discuss each employee's progress over the immediately preceding period, to determine if and how improvements can be made, and to plan to cope with the requirements of the following period, identifying any training requirements at the same time. The use of this discussion to encourage open and two-way communication and a joint agreement of future priorities and requirements should not be underestimated.

12. In the event of there being items that most people would construe as BAD NEWS (e.g. laying off staff, redundancy, etc.) every effort will be made to consult with those employees affected individually, and their representatives collectively, at an early a stage as is possible. Alternatives suggested by employees will be investigated before final decisions are made.

Note

BRIEFING GROUPS, DISCIPLINARY INTERVIEWS, PRESENTATIONS, TELEVISION and VIRTUAL MEETINGS are all used by a variety of employers to carry out the principles and practice envisaged in such a policy.

General Meetings

Introduction

Limited liability companies are required to hold meetings of their shareholder owners annually (and not more than 15 months after a previous annual general meeting) so that their directors can give account of their actions and their stewardship of the company's assets and business. Whilst in practice in most cases such a meeting tends towards 'rubber stamping', in theory, as well as in practice in more than a few instances every year, such a meeting can generate real angst and disputes as directors are called to account by those who legally appoint them and can, subject to certain requirements, dismiss them. The General Meeting of a company may be the only occasion on which the company is on public display and it is important that as well as the legally required business being transacted the company portrays itself to advantage.

Exercising control

Whilst their scope for forcing change on the directors may be limited, shareholders do have the right to ask questions at General Meetings and can, since they usually have one vote for every one share, if they have sufficient support, vote down certain business. Ultimately, this could entail removing the directors. The Department of Trade and Industry has recently conducted a consultation exercise, the results of which may well be incorporated into a new Companies Act, seeking to find views regarding the possibility of extending the shareholders' rights to require General Meetings to consider business that they wish to raise.

Convening

General Meetings are usually convened by the Secretary acting in accordance with the instructions of the Board and giving the required notice. The Annual General Meeting requires 21 days' clear notice (20 days in Scotland) although non-business days count towards the total. However, companies quoted on the Stock Exchange are now required to give their shareholders 20 working days' notice (i.e. excluding weekends and Bank holidays). An Extraordinary General Meeting requires 14 days' notice (although since some resolutions requiring consideration at an EGM require 21 days' notice sometimes the longer notice will need to be given). In addition, holders of 10 per cent or more of the shares can also require the directors to convene a meeting to discuss business which they have resolved. The 'days' notice' referred to above means clear days excluding the day of posting and the day of the meeting (although in Scotland the day of posting can be counted as Day 1).

Agenda

The Agenda for an AGM is usually contained within the Report and Accounts issued by the company, consideration of the results contained in which are usually the first item of business at the meeting.

Example

NOTICE
is hereby given that the
[number] Annual General Meeting of
[Full name of Company] Limited
will be held on [Date] at [Time] at [Address]
for the purpose of considering the following business:

1. to receive the notice of meeting and any apologies for absence;
2. to receive and adopt the Directors' report for the year ended 31 December 2000;
3. to receive and adopt the Profit and Loss a/c for the year ended 31 December 2000 and Balance Sheet as at that date and approve the payment of a dividend of [detail – amount and date];
4. to appoint directors as follows:
   a) Mr A. Bloggs was appointed a director on 1 October 2000 and retires and, being eligible, offers himself for re-election;
   b) Mr C. Bloggs and Mrs D. Bloggs, retire by rotation in accordance with Article X of the company's Articles of Association and being eligible offer themselves for re-election;
5. to reappoint Messrs Tickit and Add, who have confirmed their willingness to continue in office, as Auditors;
6. to authorise the directors to agree the remuneration of the Auditors.

On behalf of the Board

S. Bloggs
Secretary   30 March 2001

A member entitled to attend and unable to do so may appoint a proxy to vote in his/her place. Such proxies should be sent to the Registered Office of the company to arrive not later than 48 hours before the commencement of the meeting.

The AGM business

The ordinary business usually considered at an AGM is:

The accounts, balance sheet and report of directors

The shareholders have no right of approval of the accounts. Even if they 'refuse to accept' (or even 'reject' them) the accounts must still be filed with the Registrar of Companies.

Approval of final dividend

The Board can authorise and pay interim dividends on their own authority, but final dividends must be approved by the shareholders who can approve, reduce or reject (but not increase) them.

Appointment/re-appointment of directors

That is, consideration of the re-election of any director appointed since the last general meeting and of the re-election of directors retiring by rotation if required to do so by the Articles.

Appointment/re-appointment of auditors and authorising the directors to agree their payment

Any other matters required to be considered at an AGM require detailed resolutions to be set out in the Notice of the Meeting.

Running the meeting

General Meetings can have a high profile and it is important that such events run smoothly and show the company in a good light. Adequate preparation will be necessary. This can be considered in three parts:

- planning the logistics;

- BRIEFING THE CHAIRMAN;
- preparing for problems.

A. Planning the logistics

Items required:

- attendance book
- members list
- proxies
- statutory books
- directors' service contracts
- documentation for poll (see below).

The Meeting must proceed smoothly, or, in the event of adverse questioning/comment, the intervention must be handled with diplomacy, control and an awareness of the facts. This aim will only be achieved by meticulous preparation of and attention to detail well in advance of the meeting itself.

Item	Responsibility
Decide date and time	Board
Visit venue, check facilities	Co. Sec/Board
Check:	
• room and overflow facility	
• air conditioning/ventilation	
• acoustics/amplification	
• accommodation including catering/toilets	
• notice boards/room directions/signing in tables	
• display tables/pin or felt boards	
Stipulate	
• timetable for arrivals	
• serving tea/coffee/lunch (if required)	
• likely departure	
Book venue (6–12 months ahead)	Co. Sec
Delegate items to staff, e.g.	
• Greeting arrivals	Mr X
• Ensuring arrivals sign in	Miss Y
• Ushering to seats	Mr Z
• Care of Register and proxies/teller (in event of poll)	Mr A
• Statutory books, service, contracts, Minute Book	Co. Sec.

• Liaison with catering	Miss B
• Checking proposers/seconders arrive	Miss Y
• Display of products/tour of premises	Mr C
Chairman's crib	Co. Sec.
Answers to awkward questions	Board/Co. Sec. plus Merchant Bank, Solicitors

Meeting scenario for Board and advisers.
Liaison with Auditors, Solicitors, Brokers, Public Relations Co. Sec
Transport arrangements (i.e. parking may be difficult Transport
so ferrying the Board and advisers may be necessary) Manager or
suitable person

B. Documentation to be prepared
attendance cards – for companies with large numbers of shareholders, these are sent with the proxy and shareholders are requested to indicate if they intend attending;
admission cards – this enables security and recording requirements to be effected more easily.

Proxy card

Somewhat confusingly the word 'proxy' has three meanings. It is the name given to the person appointed by the shareholder to act in his place, the card which actually appoints such an agent and the act of voting:

- any and all members can appoint a proxy to act on their behalf;
- someone acting as a proxy need not be a member;
- proxy forms must be lodged with the company in advance of time of meeting;
- proxy forms must allow 'each-way' voting (i.e. both For and Against);
- a person acting as a proxy can speak and vote at a private company meeting;
- a person acting as a proxy will form part of quorum if articles allow;
- a person acting as a proxy can demand a poll (so that voting strength can be exercised).

Voting

Normally, voting is by show of hands and a simple majority is required. However, when voting by show of hands a shareholder has only one vote irrespective of the number of shares they own. Accordingly, most companies allow proxies to act on behalf of shareholders, in which case shareholders usually have one vote for every share (although the Articles should be checked to ensure this is the case).

Checklist

Administration
1. Reference should be made to the Articles of Association to check quorum, attendance and any special rules re voting.
2. If a large number are expected and/or attend the meeting it may be helpful to arrange shareholder seating in blocks of (say) 100 and to arrange for representatives of (say) the company lawyers to take responsibility for a block of seats each. The use of such representatives (announced by the Chairman at the commencement of the meeting) seeks to show that an independent force is in control of the numbers.

Note

Scrutineers may also act as receptionists, asking shareholders sign in, checking their voting strength and ensuring only shareholders sit in 'shareholder areas' to aid ease of counting.

Show of hands
1. Once a show of hands vote is required each scrutineer should note the result from his/her section and hand it to the Chief Scrutineer (two such persons may be advisable for checking purposes) to provide the Chairman with totals.
2. A poll can usually be demanded or called by:
   • the Chairman;
   • any two members (which includes representatives of corporate shareholders); or
   • any member(s) holding 10 per cent or more of the share capital.
3. Refer to the Articles for guidance regarding calling and administering a poll. The Chairman needs to:
   • check that the person making the demand has the required authority;
   • appoint scrutineers to administer the poll; and
   • set date, time, and place for poll to be taken.
4. Scrutineers can be arranged before the meeting as set out above. Since proxies are usually required to be deposited 24 hours or more prior to the Meeting, the first task of the scrutineers is to check

these proxies for authenticity and voting strength for each resolution. Proxies should provide a space for the insertion of the number of shares/votes applicable.

5. At the meeting the list of proxies lodged must be compared with those shareholders present to ensure there is no double counting. For example a shareholder has a right, even having lodged a proxy, to attend the meeting. Clarification of the authority of the proxy (is he to act or will the shareholder act in person?) needs to be sought.

6. On receiving a demand for a poll to be taken the Chairman usually has authority to require it to be conducted immediately, or at the end of the meeting or at some other date (in which case the meeting may have to be adjourned). Once again the Articles should be researched for guidance.

7. If a poll is demanded then the proxy cards provide voting cards for those not present in person. Additional voting cards (identical in most respects to the proxy card) need to be made available for those shareholders present at the meeting. Each scrutineer responsible for a shareholder seating area, should distribute voting cards to shareholders present and not represented by a proxy – and after voting collect and total them. The results from each area should be passed to the Chief Scrutineer(s) who will summarise the returns and pass the result to the Chairman, to declare the result.

A meaningful presentation

The report of the Hampel Committee on Corporate Governance recommended that directors should use the opportunity of the AGM to make a presentation concerning the company. Were this suggestion to be adopted it would convert what is very often an empty 'rubber stamping' of the Board's activities (and attended poorly as a result) into a far more meaningful meeting and a real exercise in accountability. It would also restore the purpose of the meeting in terms of providing guidance as to the future rather than, as at present, concentrating on activities and figures some of which can be as much as 18 months old.

Positive interfacing

The original concept of the AGM was that the directors would have to give personal account of their stewardship to those that appointed them. The power of self-perpetuating Boards has tended to negate the 'giving account of stewardship' aim, but nevertheless there are times when the shareholders strike back.

Case study: *Shareholder power*

1. The Hanson Group had to take into account shareholder reaction when the company sought to change its Articles of Association. The company wanted to make it more difficult for the shareholders to ask questions at the AGM, to nominate directors and to propose their own resolutions for consideration at the AGM. There was a groundswell of opposition, some from private shareholders, but mainly from institutional shareholders such that the company did an about-turn and abandoned the proposals.

2. Marks and Spencer were similarly embarrassed in the mid-1990s at a new Chairman's first AGM not only when, as the *Financial Times* commented, he 'fluffed a few resolutions' (one reason for preparing a script as outlined in BRIEFING THE CHAIRMAN), but also when a shareholder demanded to know why she could not buy a swimsuit in the company's branch in the seaside resort, Margate. The answer was that the town had been 'moved inland' by the chain's ordering computer and the Chairman dealt with the question with appropriate humour and humility. Had the Chairman known the problems facing the company that were to emerge to cut short his own chairmanship within a short time he might have insisted that a greater degree of common sense and a less corporate arrogance was what the company needed. 'Retail is detail' and basic questions like these encapsulate part of the point of making directors answerable.

Other company's that have experienced dislocation at their AGMs include:

3. British Gas. Considerable criticism of the substantial increase in the Managing Director's salary. This followed the media outcry when this increase was announced in the same week as 2,000 redundancies of the workforce.

4. Shell. One meeting was disrupted by protests following the media publicity concerning the company's environmental record in Nigeria, whilst another was disrupted when it was picketed by a marketing agency claiming the company had used its promotional ideas in a campaign although it had not been paid for them.

5. Renault. Employee shareholders used the AGM as a public platform to argue that their wage demands should be met – the meeting degenerated into a 'farce' and 'catastrophe', according to the company.

6. Greenpeace. An AGM of the pressure group was held in what was described by a national newspaper as a 'lavish' environment. Some companies might find this a consolation having been on the receiving end of pressure exerted by the group – particularly as in some cases (e.g. the Brent Spar oil platform) the basis of the anti-company feeling was later proved to be incorrect.

The problem here is not so much whether the argument is right or wrong as how to get the correct message across – and above all to be prepared for such awkward questions and disruption.

Hostility

Introduction

The effectiveness of a meeting depends on team effort. Properly led by the Chairman and with a clear sense of purpose and time, the meeting members should become a team where the output of the whole is greater than the sum of the output of the individuals. Without abandoning the formality of a meeting with an AGENDA so that the encounter becomes a BRAINSTORMING session, nevertheless the interaction of the individuals can generate original ideas and benefit all involved. Hostility within a meeting destroys this since almost inevitably empathy, rapport and co-operation will disappear and the entity can become fragmented. It is important that hostility is dealt with firmly and swiftly.

Perception of the problem

Even in the most convivial and successful environment, hostility and dissent may surface from time to time. An efficient Chairman should be able to sense that hostility may surface and, more importantly, must prepare for it. Thus if antipathy or hostility is expected ideally the initiative should be taken – for example, by meeting those with opposing views and attempting to reach a compromise agreement before it surfaces within the meeting. It is particularly important to deal tactfully yet firmly with hostility when this surfaces within an external and/or high-profile meeting.

Checklist

1. Identify the source and ensure they have a right to attend (e.g. at a General Meeting), if not deny them access. (The danger of this must be considered – after all within the meeting hostile parties are subject to some control and their accusations can be rebutted, whereas outside the meeting they can make claims without challenge – particularly if the media are present.
2. Monitor arrivals – arrange for security personnel to be nearby to deal with any physical disruption. Some of those who are hostile do not simply wish the meeting to arrive at different conclusions from

those expected, but will actually cause physical interruptions particularly using 'media-interesting' tactics to gain attention.

3. Canvass proxies sufficiently to ensure overcoming any potential opposition. If sympathetic delegates cannot be present at least their voting support should be able to be relied upon.

4. Prepare a list of the questions least wished to be asked – and a crib of suitable – and convincing answers. Those developing the questions should be encouraged to be as obtuse and awkward as possible to try to avoid those needing to reply to such questions being wrong-footed by them. No matter how unfair the question, an inability to give a convincing answer will reflect badly not on the questioner but on the respondent.

5. Brief the meeting members of the source of the problem and the steps taken to control or deal with it. All involved should know of the potential problems so that they are not taken aback should hostility surface.

6. Brief tame media contacts and provide media-trained spokesmen to answer follow- up queries. Following an awkward question with a sympathetic one may have the effect of blunting the apparent hostility as well as showing that not all present share that feeling.

7. If the hostile wishes to make a point, he should be allowed such a courtesy, answering the points made as far as possible and offering subsequent discussions if this is feasible. It may be preferable to let the person speak to 'draw the sting' rather than attempting to silence, which will only aggravate the target and may win him support from uncommitted persons.

Internal antagonism

Whilst external hostility is occasionally inevitable and can be endured, constant antagonism within (for example) a Board can be destructive and counter-productive. Whilst some argument and even disagreement can be an effective way of forcing consideration of alternatives and testing support for initiatives, if there is constant opposition for little real purpose this needs to be eradicated. Those who are likely to oppose need to be dispersed, and not to the far corners of the discussion table, as this may enable them to regroup and even solicit support from uncommitted members. If there are three, then at least one, preferably the leader, should be seated very near the Chairman. This may enable the latter to control or even silence his opposition. If the meeting uses the principle of the House of Commons (where before they can speak members have to catch the Speaker's eye) so that to speak the Chairman has to grant permission, even if only by the briefest of nods, then the person located nearest the Chairman will have the greatest difficulty, by sheer juxtaposition, in catching his close neighbour's eye.

Other opposition members need to be spread amongst supporters of the business. In this way, their apparent strength or weight will be marginalised, they will find it difficult to communicate between themselves, which may be necessary in order to re-group or seek an alternative tactic. In addition, if they are each seated next to a strong supporter of the business, the opposition may feel inhibited about making their protest at all, or continuing it in the face of experienced or heavy opposition. This echoes the principle of the appointment of non-executive directors to the Board of Directors of public companies. Since one such objective director, asking questions that executive members least want asked may feel inhibited about making his presence felt, the recommendation is at least two should be appointed. In this way they can provide moral and vocal support to each other and become a force to be reckoned with.

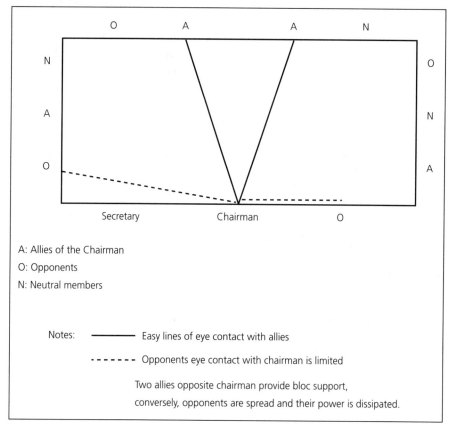

Figure 4 Dividing the opposition – to rule

Detractors

Not all of those who can reduce the effectiveness of a meeting are necessarily quite as hostile as those envisaged above. Nevertheless in terms of them negating the aim they need to be treated as hostiles.

Checklist

1. Talkers. Those not accustomed to meetings may not realise that only one conversation should be taking place – their side-discussion may be distracting to others and should be stopped. Inviting them to share their point may either force them to stop or to make the contribution for the consideration of all.
2. Over-talkers. If their output is positive and effective obviously it needs to be received. If not they need to be silenced if only to encourage others to contribute.
3. Ramblers. Again it may be that their input is valuable but it needs to be summarised and refocused. Similarly, those unable to express themselves clearly should be helped by the Chairman restating what he thinks they said and asking for confirmation.
4. Red herring fishers. These must be stopped immediately or the meeting may be hijacked to discuss an irrelevance.
5. Question-masters. These individuals can sometimes seek to dominate the meeting (the Chairman must not allow this to happen and must seize it back) by repeatedly asking questions rather than making contributions. The Chairman should request, once initial fact-finding questions have been answered, that positive contributions only will be considered.
6. Know-alls. Their knowledge should be harnessed and used. However if they seek to overawe the meeting, the Chairman should be prepared to turn questions back on them. Once caught out they may rein in their display of knowledge.

Dissent

Members of a Board who having opposed a particular item of business and presumably been outvoted have the right to have their dissent (not simply the fact that they voted against the matter) noted in the MINUTES of the meeting. Often the Chairman will attempt to avoid this step since there is then a permanent record of the split in the body, but nevertheless the member has the right and failing to agree to insert such dissent in the minutes would be a breach of this right.

Impromptu meetings

Introduction

Most of the suggestions made in this book relate to meetings which are more or less formal and follow an AGENDA regardless of whether the document convening the meeting is referred to as such or not. Not all meetings – in fact the vast majority – take place within such a formal arrangement. Most occur when A meets B by accident or design and they proceed to discuss items of common interest. This is just as much a meeting as the formal Annual General Meeting of the largest Public Limited Company in the land. The difference is that there may be little time for preparation and thus the encounter may not generate the ultimate outcome required.

Reality of the situation

It is said that the best committee is a committee of one, since in that way the ideas of the sole participant will normally be swiftly processed by virtue of their total and personal commitment. Similarly, the best meeting may be a physical meeting of two. Such a meeting satisfies the basic needs of communication, that is a two-way flow allowing each party to generate and receive feedback and to check the other's comprehension of the messages being imparted, and to gain further input from the other party immediately. Provided there is consensus, this flow should generate a dual commitment to the decision.

If we take the example of the meeting of A and B, there is little doubt that the aims of both parties may be best assured of success if they actually meet, not just discuss the subject on the phone. Eye contact and body language are important and cannot be substituted for on the phone, although the advent of videophones and video conferencing (see VIRTUAL MEETINGS) may well change this. There are other advantages, particularly to the instigator of the one-to-one meeting. Taking the example of A and B meeting but where this did not occur by chance but because A deliberately and without B knowing it set up the circumstances by which he would 'unexpectedly meet' B:

a)   In instigating the meeting, A has control of the discussion and the subject matter. He has his aims firmly in view, but must accept that in order to achieve them he must convince B of the value of those views.

b) A, one assumes, having taken the initiative, will be prepared for the encounter and thus has a better chance of manipulating his desired result than B, who is being forced to react without any advance planning. In fact, B might be wise to request time to consider any proposal before committing himself.

c) A also has control of the tactics of the meeting and can decide time, place, duration, and so on.

Staging the decision

In waylaying B to ensure the decision is taken rather than deferring it to a multi-member meeting, A has a number of devices which he can use to further his aims:

Checklist

He can:

1. prepare all arguments and facts supporting the case;
2. consider in advance all possible counter-arguments that B is likely to put forward and prepare defences or counter-arguments;
3. consider alternatives which, whilst not ideal, may be acceptable to both parties as a fall-back compromise, in order to ensure there is at least a substitutional decision acceptable to both parties (the BATNA concept used in NEGOTIATION – that is the 'best alternative to a negotiated agreement');
4. if any loss of face would be involved on B's part, consider ways to avoid this. If face-saving is attempted, that is there is a concern shown by the instigator to protect the 'reputation' of the opponent, this may help win over the opponent; indeed, recognition by B of this fact may create a rapport;
5. use devices that apply pressure on B to agree;
6. guide B to make a suggestion which A himself can then take up as 'B's idea' and agree to, which again may have the effect of gaining B's commitment. Granting recognition of the other's point of view can be a very effective manipulative tactic;
7. if B's agreement to either the desired result or the substituted result is apparently not forthcoming, a subtle threat of the need to bring the matter up at a meeting might also create sufficient pressure to gain agreement.

Create an acceptance ambience

By determining that a meeting will occur, A can also attempt to create circumstances whereby B is conditioned to accept. Thus visiting B in his domain, particularly if A is his senior, not only pays B a compliment, but also retains the initiative to the instigator to withdraw should the encounter begin to take too much time. B can hardly withdraw as it is his office.

Similarly, visiting B in his domain but just before an appointment which A knows B must keep, might put pressure on B to agree more swiftly than would otherwise have been the case to free himself from the current meeting to make the appointment. In addition, in visiting B, A can exert latent pressure if he remains standing. This exercises a dominance over the encounter and also gives the impression of immediacy – that is, 'this shouldn't take too long so I won't bother to sit down'. This places B under pressure to agree quickly.

Alternatively, arranging to meet on 'neutral ground' but in less than comfortable surroundings, can also bring pressure to bear on B to agree, particularly if he is a person who likes his creature comforts. Holding the session in A's office, puts pressure on B if he is junior to A. A further dimension to this concept can be achieved by holding the session in the Board room, or similar 'high-powered' location, and using the 'awe' of the location to affect the more junior person.

Stalling

If agreement is not forthcoming and it seems that B is resisting all coaxing, a suggestion that the matter be thought over prior to another session, at a fixed time on the following day, may create pressure for agreement. In the meantime A might be able to use a third party to promote the cause.

And what of B?

The foregoing makes suggestions that might enable A to force acceptance of his suggestion or requirement. Meanwhile B, if he is opposed to the idea is in the difficult situation of being put under pressure to discuss a matter concerning which he had no advance knowledge and thus no time to prepare. His defences are somewhat limited, particularly if he is junior to A.

Checklist

He could:
1. plead pressure of work to delay or defer consideration of the matter having first established what this is;
2. say that he needs to think about the matter;

3. state that he needs to research data and implications;
4. refer to a third party and ask whether their input has been sourced;
5. query some salient facts which might require checking or A to rethink the whole matter;
6. plead a pressing engagement which cannot be deferred;
7. or, if all else fails, feign illness!

Induction

Introduction

First impressions make a considerable impact and employers have only one chance to make a first impression. The way newcomers to the organisation are treated is all-important since research indicates that a majority of failed recruitments occur within the first year of employment – indeed recent research indicates that not only do 10 per cent of newcomers not complete their first day's work, a further 14 per cent leave within their first week and a further 17 per cent within their first month. That makes a total of two in five recruits failing to spend more than twenty working days with their new employer. Whilst inevitably some resignations result from a simple mismatch of the parties, others occur because not enough has been done at the first meeting with the new employee – that is how they are greeted and treated on their first day, how they are introduced to their new colleagues and the organisation, what efforts are made to ensure they settle down, and what support is given them whilst they learn the requirements of their job and begin to understand 'the way things are done around here'. A majority of recruits, regardless of what they may say to the contrary, do find it difficult to settle and to adapt. This involves a number of meetings with different persons over a much longer period than most employers allow. Obviously this has cost implications but it may be that this is money well invested since if the employee leaves within a short period the whole of the recruitment costs need to be borne again.

Joining

Most newcomers find their first few hours or days with a new employer somewhat disconcerting. Since no employers are alike, there will be a mass of customised data, rules, procedures, let alone colleagues, to learn and become familiarised with – a situation which is far more complex for a school-leaver with little or no work experience. Since first impressions are important, it seems obvious that considerable care and attention should be paid to attempting to make those who are about to join, or who have just joined, as welcome and as relaxed about the challenge as possible. To achieve the aim of welcoming and settling new recruits employers could approach the task in a structured way.

Checklist – Joiners

1. Provide during the recruitment/offer stage contract documentation, employee handbook and other information so that before the commencement date the recruit has an opportunity to familiarise himself with the rules, etc. This could be augmented by providing a means whereby questions, etc. regarding such documentation can be answered
2. Invite the newcomer to attend for a few hours prior to their start day and thus begin the process of familiarisation early.
3. Arrange for the recruit to attend at a specific time on the first morning (e.g. say 30 minutes after the normal start time) so that a designated person meets and greets them. This meeting should not be a quick handshake and trip to their department but be more leisurely to try to settle the person – possibly even offering refreshments and a brief chat.
4. Have available a checklist customised to the individual so that only items relevant to them need to be checked. P45 and ancillary documentation could be asked for at this point.
5. Have available all items that will be needed by the employee (e.g. safety clothing of the right size).
6. If mentoring is in operation, introduce the mentor who should then take over and be responsible for conducting the newcomer to their department and ensuring that a similar kind of measured and attentive welcome is given them there. The mentor should also ensure that the employee knows how to contact him.
7. Require the mentor to complete the first part of the induction checklist (see below) in the department preferably with the newcomer's immediate superior.
8. Introduce colleagues with a promise that these introductions will be repeated the following day as few people are able to retain the names of more than about six people when introduced. Introductions should be properly effected (both parties need to know the other's name) as too often only one party's name is said.
9. The mentor should meet the employee the following day to ensure that initial questions and concerns are answered and provide support in accordance with the mentoring policy and procedure as necessary.

10. A representative from the Personnel Department should check on how the employee is settling down after the end of the first week.

The impression to be created is that the organisation is pleased to have the person working with them, without appearing too oppressive. The amount of support will depend to a large extent on the type of person the subject is.

The induction process

Ideally, the full induction process should be structured and spread over the entire first year of employment as is suggested in the following checklist. Whilst this level of time investment may surprise some, the costs of recruiting, on-the-job coaching (whether structured or not), mistakes of those learning the job, and so on, are so considerable (retailers W H Smith recently calculated that it cost them around £3,000 to recruit a shop assistant) that any reduction is likely to be cost-effective.

Checklist

Stage 1
An *introduction* period covering the time from the conclusion of the final interview, the period of offer and acceptance, and up to and including arrival (see above, Joining checklist).

Stage 2
An *induction* period covering the time from arrival to, say, the end of the second month of employment, when a great deal of information must be absorbed so that the recruit can actually begin to work effectively.

Note

The adoption of such a period links with the legal requirement to provide the contract documentation by the end of the eighth week of employment.

Stage 3
An *instruction* period covering the time from the beginning of the third month to the end of first year of employment. The aim during this time is to enable the new employee to become completely at ease in their environment, increasingly productive and to prepare them for their first appraisal which may generate further training needs.

Information transfer

During each of these three stages various items need to be explained at structured and uninterrupted meetings and the recruit's comprehension checked. To ensure such comprehension certain items can be duplicated at subsequent stages as shown in the following checklist. Further ,the fact that there is constant interfacing should enable reinforcement of the requirements of rules to take place. Some rule infringements are simply a question of adopting bad habits – avoidance of which can avoid some disciplinary encounters.

Checklist

Recruit's name	Introduction	Induction	Instruction
Offer letter/confirmation	√		
Draft contract sent	√		
Handbook/rules/information	√	√ (knowledge)	√ (familiarity)
Reception			
– time	√		
– place	√		
– P45/P46	√		
– C383	√		
– SSP(1)L	√	√	
– P38(S)	√		
– Disabled person	√		
– Engagement form	√	√	
Access/clock card	√		
Toilets	√		
Changing rooms	√		
Locker key	√		
Car park pass	√		
Telephone	√		
Discount card	√		
Confidentiality undertaking	√	√	
Sickness administration	√	√	√
Fire Alarm	√	√	√
Safety matters	√	√	√
Wage advance	√		
Department introduction		√	
Local facilities (vending, etc.)		√	
Person introduction		√	
Job introduction		√	√
Timekeeping and breaks		√	

Recruit's name	Introduction	Induction	Instruction
Organisational rules	√	√	√
Departmental rules	√	√	√
Discipline and procedure	√	√	√
Grievance and procedure	√	√	√
Tour local departments		√	
Payslip		√	
Organisation chart		√	√
Relationship chart	√	√	
Training		√	√
Interrelated departments introduction		√	√
Induction course			√
Tour of premises			√
Questions	√	√	√

Notes

1. Either the immediate supervisor or mentor (see below) needs to cross tick to show that the item has been covered with the recruit. If a tick appears in more than one column, then the person responsible for each subsequent part of the process is expected to recheck knowledge.
2. Ideally, each employee should be asked to confirm that he/she has been taken through the items on each list – possibly by signing the checklist. It may help the efficacy of the process for this confirmation clause to be preceded by a warning such as 'You should only sign this form if you are sure that all the items detailed on it have been fully explained to you'. Having a signed confirmation at this stage may provide valuable evidence at any subsequent disciplinary encounter.
3. Once signed and completed, the checklist is returned to [personnel administration].

Induction course

Requiring new recruits to attend an induction course meeting 6–8 weeks after they join is also helpful. Held in a quiet, interruption-free room such a session can provide:

- the employer with an opportunity to speak to all newcomers together;
- the newcomers to ask their own questions and to hear questions from

(and answers given to) those facing similar challenges to their own regarding lack of comprehension of what is required, problems, etc.; and

- an opportunity to generate an informal dialogue between both parties on matters of general interest (products, processes, rules, social matters, etc.).

Such a session not only provides an opportunity to check comprehension and awareness of the rules and requirements and to run through any which are not generally understood, but also in general starts the formal communicative process by identifying the actions and attitudes expected of employees.

Keeping lists of who attended induction courses, or noting on each employee's file when they did so, provides supporting evidence of an opportunity to suggest that the employee must have known what was expected of them should any disciplinary encounter then arise.

Informal induction

The foregoing sets out the principles and practice of a structured and formal induction process. However, during every day of most newcomers' first year, there will be information to absorb, procedures to be explained and understood, and guidance to interpret. Advice and support should be provided informally at all times – not simply when a checklist requires it. This is a basic task of management.

Mentoring

As an additional method of making it easy for a recruit to learn all about the organisation and to be assimilated by it and to ensure that the possibility of disciplinary encounters is minimised, mentors may be used. The concept of a mentor is somewhat akin to an *eminence gris* – a powerful guiding force which remains in the background – although it has also been described as a 'mother hen' process, and perhaps the true description lies somewhere between the two. The essential need is for someone to keep an eye on the recruit, to be on hand to answer their questions or concerns, and to guide them with both information and advice on the way 'things are done around here' on an informal assistance basis.

Note

Few gardeners worthy of the name would plant a shrub or seedling and leave it to fend for itself. Knowing how difficult it can be for some

---

plants to become established, most conscientious gardeners will tend to check the new item regularly – ensuring it has water, shade or sun as required, is kept free from choking weeds and protected from frost. It is said that some talk to their plants and even that the plants respond. It is more likely that the plants respond simply since, in order to talk to it, the gardener has to visit it and in visiting it the essentials as set out above for strong growth are likely to be addressed. (Conversely, but similarly, it is stated that if a baby is not held and shown love it will shrivel and die.)

So too should it be with newcomers to the organisation except that, man being a communicative being, most newcomers will welcome the chance of a meeting and the conversation – genuine interest from a manager and the chance to respond could well be the reason for deciding to stay. Many employers report that the highest incidence of labour turnover occurs amongst those that have a year or less service. If newcomers are left to their own devices, it is hardly surprising that they gain misconceptions, make mistakes and feel uninvolved and even unwanted.

Interviews

Introduction

The recurrent theme of considering the various encounters in this book is the need to prepare. Nowhere is this more essential than in contemplating an interview. The fact that many interviews – particularly recruitment interviews – may start without sufficient preparation may be compounded in some cases by interviewers not appreciating that whilst it is vital that they find out as much as possible about the applicant, it is as important for the applicant to find out as much as possible about the organisation. Preparation is all-important not least since nowadays there is so much legislation proscribing how such an interface may be conducted (e.g. to avoid discrimination in its many forms).

First considerations

In contemplating recruitment, to effect which the interview is still by far the most used process, many organisations seem to overlook that:

- it is relatively easy to recruit;
- it is less easy to recruit well;
- it is far less easy to recruit well and gain the appropriate person.

In addition:

- recruiting the wrong person can lead to morale and disciplinary problems. If the wrong person is put in the job they will be under pressure to perform, may well perform badly and thus may finish up being investigated under the CAPABILITY process and ultimately, in the absence of any improvement the DISCIPLINARY process;
- dispensing with the services of employees can be expensive. Even if every effort is made to terminate employment fairly and with every consideration for the susceptibilities of the employee, it is not a happy event, and may be watched by other employees with concern on the basis 'there but for the grace of God go I';
- dispensing with services unfairly can cost up to £50,000 (the penalty for unfair dismissal having been raised under the Employment Relations Act 1999).

Research carried out on interviews does not make encouraging reading since it indicates appointments following a one-to-one interview have a high failure rate. Interviews where there is a panel have a much higher success rate although their use tends to be infrequent mainly due to time pressures or, in smaller organisations, the non-availability of suitable interviewers. Further research indicates that:

a) if several people individually interview the same selection of candidates, the results can vary widely;

b) experience in interviewing does not improve the chances of success – experienced interviewers achieved no better success rate than the inexperienced;

c) if the interviewer has not prepared for the interview then they may tend to talk too much, leaving the interviewee to talk too little and reducing the chance of obtaining information crucial to the appoint/don't appoint decision;

d) many interviewers make a decision within four minutes of the start of the interview, which must inevitably reduce their objective consideration of information sourced later in the interview particularly as many then slant their subsequent questions in favour of the decision they have already reached;

e) many interviews are unable to dispel the 'halo' effect (i.e. a favourable first impression which may be based on subjective assessment rather than objective consideration of facts – particularly those that emerge later in the interview);

f) an interviewer's personal like/dislike of a candidate affects the overall evaluation;

g) many interviewers rate female applicants lower than male applicants in traditional male-dominated jobs.

> **Note**
>
> Both f) and g) have serious potential liability implications in terms of discriminatory attitudes.

Improving the statistics

This background (based on information supplied by Coventry Business School) should prompt a need for the interviewer to prepare adequately for an interview, the key to which is information, preparation and recognition of their own prejudices. The interviewer who prepares for the encounter, recognises their own prejudices and has available as much information as possible is likely to make a more informed decision than one with no planning. Information emanates from a variety of sources.

Checklist

1. The organisation needs to generate information concerning the job to be done and the best view of the type of person that can do it. Thus the preparation of a job description, person specification (and if every aspect of requirements is not covered by these two items) and an employee requisition are key.
2. All applicants should be required to complete a standard application form even if they also submit their own curriculum vitae. The advantage of this is that standard information is then available on each candidate – and in a standard order.
3. During the interviews not only should the data submitted on the application form be probed for validity and accuracy, but any additional information required sought and notes made of this to enhance the data available. As is almost inevitable note-taking during the interview improves data recall, it also helps generate focused questions.
4. References from previous employers and possible personal acquaintances may help give a guide not only to 'what the applicant did' but 'how it was done' as well as the character of the applicant. Research indicates that generally what a person has done before is a reasonable guide to what they can do in the future although this is not conclusive and does need to be checked.

Prejudices to avoid

Identifying the ranges of prejudices and preferences can help focus the attention of the prospective interviewer on the pitfalls to avoid.

Checklist

'Offputting' characteristics
1. a regional accent (although of course this may be an advantage within the region to which it relates);
2. a foreign accent;
3. failure to make eye contact (using this to reject an applicant could be discriminatory as some ethnic backgrounds require behaviour which some would view as subservient in such an environment);
4. physical unattractiveness;
5. older candidates;
6. a physical handicap (obviously this would be discriminatory if other qualifications, etc. were equal);

'Favourable' characteristics
1. constant eye contact, nodding in agreement, etc.;
2. physical attractiveness;
3. younger candidates;
4. membership of similar/same professional or other bodies as interviewer.

Basic considerations

The best interviewers are those that plan the encounter with care, divide the session into seven key areas and deal with each area in turn:

a) Breaking the ice. This could involve the formal introductions and welcome, enquiries regarding travel and finding the location, offer of refreshments and toilet facilities (if not already covered by reception staff).

b) Brief history of the organisation, the department and the position, possibly backed with a job description. Opportunity for candidates' specific questions.

c) Thorough discussion on candidate's career and experience for the position. Check against the person specification.

d) General investigation of candidate's experience checking if possible to ensure the experience and skills claimed are actually met. This may entail testing as appropriate. There may also be a need to check the reaction to career demands, relocation attitude, etc.

e) Answering the candidate's questions about the job and prospects, encouraging such questions to gauge attitude and approach.

f) Set out the next step (which may be a second interview, etc.).

Notes

a) These outline steps are reviewed in more detail below.

b) If a panel interview is envisaged the members should each review the application and between them decide which aspects of the applicant's experience and attitude they will each check. This should avoid duplication as well as any gaps in the process.

Non-interrupted discussion

It cannot be stressed too strongly how important it is that the interviewer:

a) convenes the interview at a time suitable to the interviewee (and appreciates the reality of the situation);

> **Case study:** *Lacking perception*
>
> An applicant who looked ideal on paper explained that the only way he could attend for interview was during his lunch break since he did not want his current employer to realise he was seeking another job.
>
> Almost inevitably he was late leaving to start his lunch break and a few minutes late for the interview. The interviewer was annoyed at having been kept waiting and the interview got off to a bad start and was terminated by the applicant after 30 minutes commenting that if this was the way the organisation treated people he would withdraw his application.

Key technique

Interviewers often overlook that both parties have at least an equal interest in obtaining information from the interview. Indeed it could be argued that the applicant has a greater need for information and a perception of the ethos of the organisation as, if he gets it wrong, he could be in the position of leaving a suitable position for what turns out to be an unsuitable successor position.

---

b) sets aside sufficient time for the interview, so that it can take place in an unhurried format; and
c) avoids interruptions. Not only do interruptions break the flow of the conversation that should be an essential part of the encounter but also, if the interviewer breaks off to deal with the telephone call or a visitor, the interviewee is being given a semiotic message: 'You are not as important as this other matter so I am stopping our conversation in order to deal with it.'

Scoring sheets

The generation of a scoring sheet may assist in focusing attention on key aspects or factors that are required as well as enabling ease of comparison between candidates as all the information is prepared in a similar format. Individual factors have been inserted in the following checklist for example only.

Checklist

1. Education and training	**Essential**	**Desirable**

Degree
Qualified accountant, etc.

2. Experience
5–6 years in Accounts Department
Audit experience
Computerised accounting

3. Managerial status
Operating at supervisor/managerial
   level (2–3 years)
Managing change/computerisation

4. People skills
Communication
Leadership capability
Computer-literate

5. Career
Ambition

6. Personal characteristics
Work long hours
Work under pressure
etc.

Repeat interviews

Depending on the level of seniority of the post it may be advantageous to arrange repeat interviews (even with the same interviewer) but in a different room, etc. For example, if there were two interviewers – one leading the conversation and the other making notes at the first interview – at the second the roles of the interviewers could be reversed. It is unlikely that the interviewers will have the same range of prejudices and preferences and thus carrying out a role reversal may generate a different slant on the information generated even though the participants are identical.

Running the interview

Checklist

1. A set time should be allowed and, assuming the interviewee is present, the interview should start promptly. If due to unavoidable circumstances delay is caused by the interviewer, an apology should be made and the situation updated at least every five minutes.

2. A room without a telephone, and with a facility for avoiding interruptions, should be used. Ideally interruptions should always be avoided. If, however, it is unavoidable, the situation should be explained to the interviewee, an apology should be given and the interruption minimised. If the interruption lasts longer than five minutes, updates should be given then and at least every further five minutes.

Note

In the event of lengthy delay or interruption, as well as an apology being provided, the interviewee should be given the opportunity to arrange an alternative time. Costs involved should be reimbursed.

---

3. The parties should be seated in comfortable chairs of the same height, without strong lights being used to dazzle either party.
4. The interviewer should spend a few minutes on introductory matters attempting to place the applicant at their ease. It might be appropriate to take the initiative and outline some history of the organisation, its products and position in the marketplace.
5. The bulk of the interview time should be spent obtaining information concerning the career and experience, etc. of the applicant and providing information regarding the position, requirements and prospects of the job. In this regard it is essential to use open questions ('tell me about', 'how did you cope with...' 'what was best (and worst) about...'), and so on, rather than closed questions ('did you enjoy...', 'you didn't stay there long did you'). This should ensure that the interviewee has to answer with sentences and comments rather simply replying 'yes' or 'no'. It is also essential that the interviewer is seen to 'listen' and to be attentive. Taking notes may be one way of indicating this, whereas thumbing through the papers whilst not looking at the interviewee is not – it can indicate to the interviewee a lack of interest in the answer being provided. Control of such 'body language' is essential since powerful messages are sent in this way. If the interviewee gains the impression that the interviewer is not interested they are unlikely to give of their best.
6. Where possible, check the technical expertise claimed by the interviewee. The impression should not be given that the interviewer is expert in the subject (unless, of course he is, and even then it might be better to conceal such knowledge and let the applicant speak). It may help the applicant talk if the conversation is

kept going with such comments as 'I don't know too much about this, but I thought that...'. Such gambits allow the applicant free rein to explain the point, or if the opportunity is declined, it may indicate that experience was not as wide or applicable as was previously thought.

7. Guide the conversation to the preferred route with the minimum of intervention, so that the applicant is encouraged to talk at length. During this, the applicant's knowledge can be better displayed and better tested. This part of the interview should take the form of a discussion about the vacancy and the applicant's suitability for it. It should be objective and attempt to avoid any judgemental overtones – talents and experience vary from person to person. An interview should not be an assessment of whether the applicant is 'up to the job', but whether the requirements of the organisation and the attributes and attitude, skills and experience of the applicant, represent a match with such requirements.

8. For certain vacancies (e.g. assemblers, word-processing operators, cashiers, etc.) where technical skills are essential, it may be appropriate to arrange a short 'hands-on' test.

9. Every opportunity should be afforded to the interviewee for them to ask questions on any topic related to the [organisation], vacancy, prospects, etc.

Concluding the interview

Interviews should conclude naturally at the point that both parties feel that they have as much information about the other sufficient for their purpose. For most positions this is unlikely to be less than thirty minutes after the start of the interview, and for supervisory and more senior positions, less than sixty minutes, bearing in mind that in recruiting for such positions it will be normal to invite applicants for a second (and further) interview(s).

At the end the interviewer should state the position regarding the recruitment. This could be:

a) that the applicant is not suitable to be considered further – in which case they should be told so immediately;

b) that a shortlist is being prepared and the applicant is likely (or not) to be placed on such a shortlist and will be required to attend for further interview. Usually there will be a need for the interviewee to be contacted at a later date with the decision. If so then a date by which time they will be contacted should be given. It is essential, having given such a date, that it is adhered to (even if the call is only to defer further the date/decision);

c) that the applicant is required to return for further interview possibly by another interviewer. In this case if possible a date should be set;
d) that a decision will be made within a set time and the interviewee will be contacted. Again whatever date is given should be adhered to;
e) that the interviewee is entirely suitable and is to be offered the position.

Grading and comparison

Interviewing is said to be an imprecise science – in fact, it is probably not a science at all since with the best attention the interviewer will still conclude with a view which must have, despite every endeavour, some elements of subjectivity. This can be compounded with multi-applications where comparison is required.

It may assist data collation and applicant comparison to use a grading form attempting to evaluate characteristics. If each characteristic has to be 'scored' and the same interviewers see the same candidates, some degree of comparison is possible (although the negative and positive characteristics set out above may still be applicable). If instead of seeing the applicants individually the interviewers see them as a panel and discuss their grading before recording it this may help move the assessment to a more objective view.

This is a somewhat mechanistic approach to the task and could be refined by weighting certain items so that those perceived to be of greatest value are scored more highly than those perceived to be of less value. Thus if three years' auditing were essential this might score 10, whereas communication skills were not thought to be as essential a requirement might only score 1. The excellent communicator with only one year auditing would then score substantially less than the poor communicator with five years' auditing experience, and so on.

Reducing the requirements to this kind of form has two added benefits:

a) each candidate is made more memorable as a person; and
b) the candidates can be compared more easily and more objectively than would otherwise be the case.

Note

The advent of technology is causing reconsideration of the methods of applicant interviewing. An increasing number of organisations are using telephone interviews at least as a first stage in the process for more senior appointments. Applicants surveyed seem, however, to give less good an account of themselves when being interviewed over the phone. It has been suggested that this is because being at home they

---

157

are dressed and posed informally and have not adopted the 'professional' approach they would in the interviewer's office. Virtually simultaneously a product has been developed that enables a caller to tell whether the other party is telling the truth or not. This could be of considerable assistance bearing in mind a substantial proportion of applicants do lie during job interviews.

Finally, in the USA increasingly organisations are using their WEBSITE to display details of the job and career opportunities they have available to all site visitors. Job seekers, particularly those at university, can access the website of the organisation via the university's computer and because that part of the site is interactive, can 'complete' a job application form and await further contact by the organisation.

Meatless meetings

Introduction

There are a number of organisations where one could be excused for believing that the managers spend all their time in meetings and very little time dealing with their number one priority – leading their teams. One must hope that productive decisions do emerge from such meetings and that they are not as does seem to happen in more than a few cases, simply an opportunity for an individual, charged with taking decisions, to submerge his responsibility within the collective decision of the 'meeting'. In addition it appears that some such meetings seem to achieve little more than a chance for the participants to socialise. Either by accident or design such meetings have become 'meetings without meat' or meatless meetings – the event remains even whilst the purpose has long since departed. A further refinement can involve part of the meeting degenerating from a purposeful discussion to a purposeless agenda item – retained since no one has considered its purpose. There are two challenges here – to make the meatless meeting effective (or disband it) and to make the meatless member effective (or similarly remove them).

Losing the plot

Before any meeting is convened the question 'is there a way of dealing with the problem without needing to convene a meeting?' needs to be put and answered – and put and answered not just for the initial meeting but regularly thereafter.

Case study: *Losing its point – 1*

> A committee was set up to run a social club and originated and gained approval for a constitution. It found premises and appointed a working leader. In appointing the leader, virtually all the duties and responsibilities formerly undertaken by the committee were transferred to him; nevertheless the committee

> continued to meet. Virtually to justify its existence, it then required the leader to report to it each month, even though all the meeting members were involved as club members and knew every development.

Key technique:

The original purpose of the committee had been exhausted, but until this was realised it continued to meet.

Since experience shows that a large number of purposeless meetings or 'meetings without meat' are held, one objective of challenging the existence of all such meetings should be to ensure that each does have sufficient 'meat', and indeed 'meat' of the correct flavour, to warrant convening or continuation. Sadly meetings are often held:

a) lacking any real purpose, simply because it is either a matter of habit or is an easy way out of the decision-making process;

b) for the wrong reason(s) which will automatically generate the wrong decisions (some meetings seem almost to be held for the personal aggrandisement of some of the members);

c) as a method of shifting responsibility from an individual to a collective basis.

Note

Since there is a widespread tendency to promote above the level of competence – the Peter Principle – which results in managers being expected to operate at one level above that for which their talents and experience suit them, this may encourage over-promoted managers to protect their positions by seeking a meeting to take responsibility for decisions which are properly their own.

d) as a delaying or spoiling tactic. If a swift decision is essential for the success of the project, deferral to a meeting may either kill it off, or ensure that its success is marred or rendered impossible;

e) as a means of achieving a 'hidden agenda', that is moving towards a decision which has an effect additional to those visible and recognised by most people; or

f) as a quasi-social event where the members can exchange news and gain views of the other participants.

Whereas the first five items above can be regarded as criticisms, the last is not necessarily meant as such. Although the meeting may not have an identified purpose for discussion, such an informal forum may be an essential means of its members keeping in touch and discussing developments. This can be extremely valuable, particularly where the participants are normally geographically separated and are only otherwise able to keep in touch electronically or by post. In many ways such an unconstructed meeting is akin to the type of meeting described in BRAINSTORMING, although there the event usually has an identified purpose and here it is more for the purpose of 'keeping in touch'. The inherent danger is that the initial positive benefit of such a meeting can be lost by regularity of contact and the side-tracking of the business purpose in favour of the purely social.

Case study: *Losing its point – 2*

A newly appointed manager was given a job description which included the requirement to obtain references for proposed new employees from their previous employers for fidelity guarantee insurance cover. The files were haphazard and the procedure apparently non-existent so she contacted the Personnel Department for help, only to be told, 'Oh we must have a meeting about that', which was set for two days later. This meeting, involving no fewer than eight people, was informative in terms of getting to know the people involved and, as a result of the advice provided in a somewhat haphazard way, the procedure developed solved the problem. However this could have been achieved in a ten-minute, two-party, face-to-face chat two days earlier, rather than an hour-long multi-member meeting.

Key technique:

Whilst the meeting may well have been successful in terms of building a working relationship, in terms of its real purpose, immediate guidance of a newcomer in an unclear procedure, the meeting failed. The two- or three-day delay in chasing up references from former employers could have resulted in an unsuitable applicant being offered employment. The meeting wasn't entirely without meat – simply perhaps that the 'flavour' was somewhat different from that intended.

Effectiveness requires purpose

In the AGENDA section the following definition of a meeting was suggested: 'A gathering of essential participants only, each of whom has something to contribute, to discuss a problem touching on all their interests, to arrive at certain decisions, all as required by the pre-determined aim of the meeting itself.' If every time a meeting is proposed the question 'does this meeting fit this definition?' is asked, this may help weed out meatless meetings which do otherwise fit the older definition also referred to previously – that of taking minutes and wasting hours.

A further and extremely dangerous effect of allowing meatless meetings to continue or, worse, proliferate, is not so much that the meeting members waste their time, it may well be that those that 'watch' (i.e. members of their teams) will suspect that the meeting has no meat or purpose which may, perhaps inevitably, impair their own productivity. 'If the leader is poor the team will be poor; if the leader is good the team will be good' (in fact, if there is a poor leader it is unlikely that a team will be formed at all).

Self-perpetuating meetings

Whilst a meeting may be required to determine policy or changes to policy, in which case an interplay of different views and queries may be essential, there is often a great deal which is actually little more than a review of the status quo, requiring a minimum of input from members who are required only to note and digest. The problem is that the scenario in which meeting members find themselves actually puts pressure on them to comment or question data or decisions simply to justify their presence. Indeed this can hold true even though the subject matter may be provided purely for information, and their comments are virtually irrelevant. In these circumstances, such comments may be only serving the purpose of prolonging a redundant meeting.

Case study: *Managing by exception*

A Company Secretary was required to update the Board on developments on rent reviews of a number of the company's leased properties. In view of the large number of such properties this meant that at any time he would need to report on around twenty negotiations. Very often most of the factors that would dictate a new level were outside the control of the company and, whilst his brief was invariably and understandably to achieve as low an increase as possible, market forces tended to militate against this and the company had ultimately to accept the almost inevitable increases. This agenda item began to consume between 30 and 45 minutes of each meeting, until he decided to include as part of the agenda, a synopsis of the status of each negotiation, and suggested to the Chairman that discussion only take place on an 'exception basis', that is that only where there were particular factors or facts of relevance or perceived to have been overlooked was discussion invited, the remainder being an information exercise only. Thereafter, not only did the members have a written and detailed update, rather than a verbal report, but also the time devoted to the item dropped to 10 minutes or so.

Key technique:

Advance single member research may enable the meeting's attention to be concentrated on the essentials.

Warning

 The fact that a regular item on an Agenda does not seem to merit discussion, etc., is not necessarily a good reason for omitting it. The fact that the item is reported, noted and no action is required is not indicative that no decision has been taken. In fact a decision (i.e. that no action is necessary) has been taken and the matter has been 'reviewed'. Obviously if the figures or facts reported are not in line with what was required action is needed and should be taken. However this is only possible if the information is available.

Making the meeting redundant

The process developed in this case study was later adopted for a number of other routine reports so that the 'discussion aspect' of those items was removed. This process can be used with other business often referred to a meeting for noting rather than decision. Similarly, originating procedures and checklists for policy matters will provide guidance for those required to implement decisions rather than needing Board approval on each occasion.

Case study:	*Decide policy*

The company was concerned that many long-serving employees were retiring without income, other than the state pension, as, due to a formerly restricted entry requirement, they had not been able to join the occupational pension scheme. Accordingly during a number of Board Meetings a policy and a procedure for granting ex-gratia allowances to such employees was agreed and a number of cases examined. Thereafter, however, the Personnel Department automatically calculated the entitlement and set up the payment, under a Director's authorisation. Each year the Board continued to review the system, but from a policy not an administrative angle.

Key technique:

Developing policies and procedures, checklists and guidance not only avoids the need for meetings to discuss individual cases, but also provides ongoing guidance to those who need to make decisions. The availability of criteria and checklists can negate the need for repeated discussions and should also avoid one-off solutions that may create unwanted precedents.

Backlash

Obviously reducing discussion to 'exception only' reporting may not please everyone. Some meeting members regard their membership and attendance as enhancing their prestige and position, and the length of the meeting as indicative of its, and thus their, importance. Removing routine business restricts their capacity for comment on non-essentials where they are unlikely to say the 'wrong thing'. If they cannot comment on such mundane items, then their total contribution to the meeting may be, and be seen to be, limited, which may, in turn, question their continued membership. Contributions should be examined in case the number of meeting members can be reduced which may in turn reduce the duration of the meeting. The responsibility for effecting this process is that of the Chairman. Unfortunately, not all Chairmen are effective at this type of process – which may of course be why there is a meatless meetings at all! The appointment of an ineffective Chairman is likely to be more common in social rather than business meetings but it is by no means unknown in the latter. Headed (one can hardly say led as it would be a contradiction in terms) by an ineffective Chairman, even meetings with meat can become ineffective and inefficient – whilst meatless meetings can proliferate.

Case study: *Chairman only in name*

It was obvious that the Chairman had little experience of well-run meetings, let alone chairing one. To his despair, the new member found that there was no agenda, merely a list of topics which was actually put together when the members met, no minutes or record of what had been agreed previously, and no apparent intent to address various requirements with any degree of efficiency. In addition, the meeting participants, lacking any control or leadership, spent virtually the whole meeting chatting amongst themselves as much as addressing the issues they had gathered to discuss. At his second meeting, the new member made several constructive suggestions for improving the performance generally and at his third, the Chairman did not turn up and the new member was asked to chair the meeting.

Sadly, such a situation is not always as easily resolved. Often the meeting needs to soldier on, with the Secretary and members trying to push for greater efficiency and performance against the one person who should be leading them in that endeavour!

Note

'Meetings are indispensable when you don't want to do anything.' – J. K. Galbraith (Canadian-born American economist and Professor at Harvard University)

Media and public relations

Introduction

The operations and activities of organisations (particularly those that are in any way viewed as 'suspect' or 'questionable') are increasingly subject to the attention of 'the media' and/or the public, either as stories in their own right, or as part of a larger, and possibly investigative, 'story'. Even the manner in which employees are treated can now be scrutinised and commented upon as a result of media attention to Employment Tribunal hearings of what would once have been regarded as internal matters. Whilst the incidence of such attention is greater for those organisations which are 'household names' all organisations may be subject to scrutiny – particularly if a CRISIS develops.

Assess the challenge

Since attention can arise and/or increase dramatically when a crisis in the operation occurs, all organisations should, at least, consider the need for media and public interfacing whether this is likely to take place at a pre-convened meeting or less formally over the phone, etc. Whether the responsibility for public relations is recognised or not it occurs every day. Each time a customer buys a product or service a 'public relationship' occurs. Indeed nowhere is dealing with public relations positively and constructively more vital than in handling customers and particularly their complaints. Despite this being obvious, surprisingly few organisations think of linking, however tenuously, the activities of the CUSTOMER Complaints/Care and Public Relations Departments and perhaps the most pertinent piece of advice in considering media and public relations as a discipline would be to make it responsible for dealing with customers – particularly their problems.

Reputation

Reputation and public awareness may be indefinable and incapable of quantification, nevertheless their value can be considerable. A reputation can take years to build – and just seconds to lose.

167

Most crises develop externally and when they do combine to challenge its reputation or survival, the organisation that has not prepared for this, that has not cultivated media connections or has not rehearsed for the investigative or even hostile approach, or the disaster (see CRISIS COMMUNICATION) may find it virtually impossible to counter adverse comment, or to put over its own case. A comprehensive approach incorporating policy, research, crisis reaction, training and practice is essential.

Policy

A suitable policy/procedure of which the following is a draft could be adopted:

Checklist: Media and public relations commitment

1. The organisation recognises the natural interest that will be evinced by the media on behalf of the public and the public itself in its operations and will make all information, other than that which is regarded as confidential, regularly available primarily to accredited sources.

> **Note**
>
> Such sources could include named journalists, a list of journals, newsletters, radio and TV outlets, etc. who would automatically be sent all literature produced for external use as a matter of course.

2. [Name and deputy] will act as spokesperson for the organisation and will be briefed continually by [directors/executives as applicable] those responsible for each [division, product, etc.].
3. In the event of other employees being contacted by representatives of the media, they will be referred to the spokesperson.
4. In interfacing with the media, the spokesperson will endeavour to be truthful at all times, and to ensure that such information is correctly reported.
5. Contacts with each branch of the media will be made and such contacts will be regularly briefed so that they have background knowledge of the organisation, which is then updated continuously.
6. In the event of a serious occurrence the senior manager responsible must brief the spokesperson as quickly as possible.
7. On no occasion regardless of the circumstances should the products, services or reputation of the organisation or of any

person working in it or of any third party connected with it be called into doubt or question in any way whatever without the knowledge of [name].

Research

The above policy statement covers the whole area of media/public interest in very general terms. As far as the spokesperson is concerned, however, they will need to have access to a range of data and to be in command of the latest developments. No media briefing or interview will be successful unless adequate preparation and research has been carried out. Thus the following are necessary:

a) identify the areas of operation in which the media/public could be interested;

b) identify the target audiences and the information they will require;

c) identify the nature of the interest of each part of the target audience and what information will be required;

d) establish who is to deal with the ongoing enquiry and how they are to be briefed and updated concerning progress and all related aspects;

e) encourage the spokesperson to create links with representatives of all media (establishing names, positions, main interests or 'angles', deadlines, potential bias, etc.);

f) regularly examine stories and reports concerning the organisation to ensure the (correct/required/positive) image is being created;

g) continually develop questions (and, more importantly, answers thereto) that the organisation least wants asked and become conversant with both (updated as necessary);

h) prepare and update a résumé of all the successes of the organisation so that good news is available which may be able to be used to leaven the bad.

Controlling bad news

The difficulty many organisations experience is that often the media are only interested when there is bad news mainly since they know, human nature being what it is, more people are likely to pay attention to or be attracted by 'bad news' than good. Instinctively, those 'defending' the bad news story may wish to control the dissemination of the news. This is virtually impossible in an open society. Almost inevitably the story will emerge and, if it appears that the company has been trying to stifle information, the result may be worse than if it had held up its hands in the first place. The media are acknowledged to have a very efficient spy system – aided and abetted by the public who very often know that the media are willing to pay for stories and particularly pictures.

Case study:	Everyone's a reporter
	As this section was being written a car was crashed into the gates at the end of Downing Street. Within a few hours, film footage of the incident (or at least its immediate aftermath) was being shown on national television, courtesy of a tourist who camcorded the event from the top of a bus virtually as it happened and made his film available.

During an interview concerned with bad news, particularly if it reflects poorly on the organisation, some rapport with or positive feeling from the audience may be gained if the spokesperson can introduce details of facts that show the organisation in a better light or simply acknowledges the bad news. This needs to be done with care and in appreciation of the subject matter of the enquiry. Introducing details of record production last week when the subject is the death of an employee would be crass and unfeeling and would generate entirely the wrong impression. However, mentioning that in 50 years of production on the site and in a workforce of 20,000 personnel this is the first fatality which is deeply regretted could at least, whilst not detracting from the tragic current circumstances, place the incident in some kind of perspective. Being able to state that the organisation is caring for relatives and has called an independent third party to investigate the circumstances thoroughly might also help. 'No comment' is not an option if some respect for the organisation is to be preserved.

On the contrary, 'holding one's hands up' to the offence may win some grudging admiration.

Case study:	Coming clean
	Lee Iaccocca, the man who 'saved' Chrysler, often recounts the event of the company selling cars even though it knew they had a fault and being found out for doing so. Research indicated that 55 per cent of the public thought the corporation were 'bad boys'. Chrysler ran an advertising campaign admitting their mistake and promising that it would not be repeated. Subsequently, market research revealed that 67 per cent of the public liked the fact that the corporation had 'owned up' and were in favour of it – a massive about-turn of public opinion.

Crisis reaction

Whilst briefing the media on the more mundane aspects of organisation performance may be relatively easy, dealing with such interest in the aftermath of a calamity or disaster poses considerable problems capable of being tackled only if based on contingency planning, i.e. anticipating the disaster and making advance plans for dealing with the effects (see CRISIS COMMUNICATION). The advantage of 'planning for disaster' is that lengthy and calm thought can be given to alternative tactics and reactions, without the considerable time pressure for reaction that the incidence of disaster can cause. In addition, consideration of alternative actions in the event of disaster may suggest beneficial changes in current operations. Obviously, if it is to be of value such planning must be both comprehensive and regularly updated. Accordingly it will be an expensive operation, albeit one that should be regarded as an investment – certainly trying to cope with the innumerable requirements for action and comments following a disaster without at least a little planning will be virtually impossible.

Instant reactions

There is an increasing tendency to try to obtain at least a few sentences of comment from spokespersons as they leave (for example, a meeting or building). Since this practice is widespread it should not take people by surprise yet there are instances when even those experienced in answering intrusive questions 'lose their cool'. The solution is to expect that there will be such questions and rather than exiting immediately take some minutes to consider the worst questions and suitable answers bearing in mind that although 'no comment' may not be the best answer in such circumstances, at least it will be preferable to losing one's temper. In visual terms someone saying nothing cannot be tolerated – the producer will quickly cut the sequence.

Case study:	*Not so inscrutable*
	A former head of a stock exchange in the Far East was subjected to intrusive questioning at a press conference, which was being televised live. He took such exception to some of the questions that he attempted to lean across the desk and hit the reporter. He was later imprisoned for several malpractices but even had this not occurred it could have been difficult for him to have resumed his position after such a public exhibition.

Other observers

A generation ago although news of some of the largest companies in the land would have been featured from time to time, the extent of this was tiny compared to the considerable interest evinced nowadays. This is partly as a result of the privatisation of nationally known utilities but perhaps more because of an increasing awareness of the growing power inherent in, particularly, multinational organisations. Some of these are larger in wealth terms than several Third World countries and recent proposed mega-mergers would create corporations, which are as large as some Second World countries. Interest in the operations of and personalities involved in such corporations is inevitable and such entities should be prepared to provide information to protect their reputations.

Minutes

Introduction

Control (by shareholders) and direction (by directors) of companies is exercised by meetings – General and Board Meetings. Minutes of both need to be made not only as a matter of record, but also to evidence that duties and responsibilities have been exercised as required. To be able to evidence the latter a record should be made even of 'meetings' of a single person(e.g. where there is only one shareholder or director). Although there is no obligation to hold Board Meetings it could be difficult to prove that the directors had exercised their duty of care if there is no record of decisions taken. There is no set format for minutes but it is generally accepted that minutes should record decisions only, rather than commentary, argument and/or reasons for the decisions.

General Meetings

Minutes of all General Meetings must be taken and should be filed safely either in bound or loose-leaf books (if loose-leaf the book should ideally be lockable and the pages numbered sequentially). Increasingly, minutes are being held electronically but it would be wise always to have a hard copy available – if only since an inspection can be more easily accommodated. Care should also be taken when commissioning new computers to ensure that records stored electronically on previous generations of computers can still be accessed. Shareholders have a right of access to the minutes of General Meetings (only) for two hours each business day.

The Articles should be examined to check the status of the minutes. Usually they are *prima facie* evidence of the proceedings. Ideally they should be approved and signed as a 'true record' at the next following Board Meeting (not the next following general meeting) in which case it may be difficult to challenge their validity – indeed the Articles may indicate that if this procedure is followed the Minutes may be regarded as conclusive evidence of the proceedings.

An example of a set of minutes for a General Meeting follows and in it explanatory notes appear at its conclusion. These notes correspond to the figures in round brackets on the right-hand side of the text.

Example: General Meeting minutes

ANY OTHER COMPANY LTD   431(1)
MINUTES of the [x]th ANNUAL GENERAL MEETING
held on Thursday, 8 February 2001 at [address] at 10.00 a.m.
Present: ABC (in the chair)
EFG
HIJ
KLM
NOP
12 shareholders
Apologies for absence were received from QRS, TUV and WXY
In attendance: AAA (Secretary)
BBB (Auditor)

1. NOTICE
The Secretary read the notice of the meeting   (2)

2. DIRECTORS' REPORT for the year ended 30 September 2000
The Chairman referred members to the Report and Accounts for the
year ended 30 September 2000 and the Balance sheet as at that date.
He requested Ms BBB (of accountants – name) to read the audit report
which she did.   (3)
   The Chairman proposed, NOP seconded and it was resolved
unanimously that the report and accounts of the company for the year
ended 30th September 2000 and the Balance Sheet as at that date be
and they are hereby received and adopted.   (4)

3. DECLARATION OF DIVIDEND
The Chairman referred to the payment of an interim dividend in June
2000 and to the fact that the Board were recommending payment of a
final dividend of 2p per ordinary shares. He proposed, KLM seconded
and it was resolved unanimously that on 9 February 2001, the
company should pay a final dividend in respect of the year ended 30
September 2000 of 2p per ordinary share (plus tax credit) to the
holders of ordinary shares registered on the books as at 1 January
2001.   (5)

4. RETIREMENT OF DIRECTORS
The Chairman stated that in accordance with the Articles of Association
and as set out in the notice of the meeting, Mrs EFG and Mr KLM
retired by rotation and each being eligible, had submitted themselves
for re-election. The Chairman proposed, Mr HIJ seconded and it was

resolved unanimously that the re-election of both retiring directors
could be put to the meeting as one motion.   (6)
The Chairman proposed, Mr K. Jones, a shareholder seconded, and it
was resolved unanimously that Mrs EFG and Mr KLM be and they
hereby are re-elected directors of the company.

5. AUDITORS

The Chairman referred to the need to re-elect auditors of the company.
It was proposed by Mrs EFG, seconded by the Chairman and resolved
nemo contendare that Messrs [Name] be and they are hereby re-
appointed auditors of the company until the conclusion of the   (7)
 next following AGM on terms to be agreed by the directors.
The meeting terminated at 10.25 a.m.

Chairman ....   8 March 2001 (8)

Notes

1. To aid security (and cross-referencing) every page should be
    numbered consecutively. Often minutes of General and Board
    Meetings are kept in the same folder and numbered consecutively
    as one complete record. This can be difficult should a shareholder
    wish to inspect the minutes, as although shareholders have a right
    to see the minutes of General Meetings, they have no right to see
    the minutes of Board Meetings. Thus the minutes would have to be
    separated and the numbering might look somewhat odd – and
    generate questions. Minutes of meetings of shareholders must be
    kept at the registered office, but there is no restriction regarding
    the location of minutes of Board meetings, although they should
    be kept securely.
2. There is no requirement to read the notice of the meeting but
    many companies do so – if nothing else it provides time for
    latecomers to find their seats.
3. Similarly there is no requirement for the Auditors to read the audit
    report (which they will already have had to sign) but again it does
    little harm and, at the very least, helps identify the auditor to the
    members.
4. The members can only receive accounts already approved by the
    directors; they have no legal right of approval or rejection. Strictly
    speaking under common law, when the Chairman of a meeting
    proposes a resolution no seconder is necessary. However, since few
    members may know this it may be better to arrange seconders.
    Ideally it is better to arrange for seconders to come from

shareholders who are not directors. This gives, at least, the appearance of democracy at work.

5. The members can either approve or reduce the dividend; they cannot increase it. Using a 'striking date' of some time before the meeting should enable all the calculations to be carried out and even the cheques drawn on the assumption that the dividend will be approved. Once this happens, the cheques can be signed or authorised and despatched so that members receive them on the due date. PLCs have also to notify the Stock Exchange once a dividend is approved (and indeed to give notice of a Board meeting at which the question of recommending/paying a dividend will be considered).

6. The re-election of directors en masse can only take place if the meeting have previously approved (as here) that the re-election can take place in this way.

7. *'Nemo contendare'* means that no one objected to the proposal and is often used in its shortened form – 'nem. con.'. Thus, although everyone voted in favour of all the previous proposals, in this instance, whilst no one voted against, one or more members abstained.

8. The minutes of a General Meeting should be signed by the Chairman at the next following Board meeting – i.e. there is no need to wait for the next General Meeting.

Board Meetings

Usually, the minutes of General Meetings will be fairly short and formal. However the minutes of Board Meetings may be far more complex and lengthy. Ideally, minutes should:

- be short and concise;
- comprise only a résumé of the decisions taken;
- be a true, fair and accurate record. This is particularly important in case the organisation needs to produce a certified copy of a minute to a third party, e.g. to evidence a signatory's authority to sign a contract;
- be full enough and contain sufficient information to enable an outsider to comprehend the decisions, although at times it may be necessary and/or advisable to include some commentary.

Explanatory notes appear at the end of the following example corresponding to the figures in round brackets on the right-hand side of the text.

ANY COMPANY LIMITED 182(1)

MINUTES of a
BOARD MEETING held on 8 March 2001
at [address] at 10.00 a.m.
Present: XYZ (in the chair)
ABC
DEF
GHI
In attendance: JKL (Company Secretary)
(Mr TSS, Auditor was in attendance for items covered by
minute 3 i and ii) (2)
An apology for absence due to illness was received from Mr UVW and
accepted. Those present signed the attendance book. (3)

1. MINUTES
The minutes of the Board Meeting and of the Annual General Meeting
held on 7 February 2001 previously distributed were taken as read,
approved and signed. (4)

2. SHAREHOLDER MATTERS
It was resolved that a share transfer covering 500 Ordinary shares in the
company from Mrs MNO to Mr PQR be and it hereby is approved and
that a share certificate in the name of Mr PQR be issued and the
required entries be made in the Register of Members. The Secretary
was asked to write personally to Mr PQR welcoming him as a
shareholder. Action: JKL (5)
    A report from the Company Secretary recommending that
responsibility for the share registration work of the company be placed
with Share Registrars Ltd was accepted and the terms of the contract
approved. The company secretary was requested to make the necessary
arrangements in liaison with the Chairman. Action: JKL
(Mr DEF, having previously notified the company that he had a
consultancy agreement with Share Registrars Ltd did not take any part
in this discussion or decision.) (6)

3. FINANCE
i) Management accounts
The full set of management accounts for the month of February and
the cumulative six months were tabled and discussed in detail. The
favourable comparison with budget was welcomed, as was the
Managing Director's opinion that the trading and financial situation
would continue to show improvement, both in real terms and against
budget.

It was noted that the situation regarding discounts and promotional payments was still being clarified and additional controls would be introduced from the start of the new financial year.

A number of estimated provisions were listed for possible incorporation in the year-end accounts.   Action: ABC

ii)   Depreciation

It was agreed to change the company's accounting policies so that depreciation for the current financial year would be charged on vehicles, office equipment and computers : 33.3 per cent p.a. straightline. It was noted that this change was required to be recorded in the Accounting Policies note to the next set of audited accounts.

iii) Capital expenditure
   a) It was agreed that a further five product units at a cost of around £4,000 each could be purchased on stages over the remainder of 1996 to allow the sale of [detail]. Mr UVW, whom failing the Company Secretary, would authorise each item bearing in mind the effect on cash flow.   (7)
   b) The Chairman referred to Capital Expenditure Project form number 13/01 for the investment in [detail] which projected a first year return of 14 per cent rising to 17 per cent in year 2 on a fully absorbed basis. The project was approved for implementation no earlier than 30 September 2001.   Action: ABC

iv)   Cash flow.
   The latest projection for the period ending 30 June 2002 was tabled, discussed and approved.
v)   Investigations for the replacement of the company vehicles allocated to six area managers would be carried out. The guidance of the auditors as to the company's and individual's tax situation would be sought.   Action: GHI
vi)   Bank Mandate.

The Secretary reported that the company's bankers had requested that a new mandate on the main drawing account be completed.

It was resolved that the company operate the No. 1 Main Drawing account in its name with the Finance Bank Plc on the terms and subject to the restrictions set out in a new mandate a copy of which initialled by the Chairman for the purposes of identification is attached to these minutes, and that the Secretary be and he hereby is empowered to take such actions as might be necessary to give effect to this resolution.

Action: JKL(8)

vii) Borrowings

The Secretary reported that in the absence of Mr UVW he had negotiated an additional £100,000 overdraft facility with the Finance Bank on the same terms as the existing facility. This additional borrowing was available for the 26 weeks until end August 2001. Although he had expected to receive documentation requiring Board approval to evidence this borrowing this had failed to arrive.

It was resolved that the Chairman, ABC and UVW (whom failing the Company Secretary) be and they hereby are empowered to sign such documents and take such actions to provide the company's bankers with the documentation they required in order to facilitate the advance of this additional borrowing requirement.

The Secretary was instructed to let each Board member have copies of the relevant items and documentation when these were to hand.

The Secretary confirmed that even with this additional borrowing the limits in the Articles had not been breached. (9)

Action: XYZ, ABC, JKL

4. CURRENT TRADING

The Managing Director reported that [résumé of report.........]. An analysis showing the deterioration over a five-year period of sales of the main product was tabled and it was agreed that the deadline for delivery of supplies of Project X needed to be brought forward to compensate for the expected shortfall in sales in the latter part of the calendar year. Action: ABC

DEF requested that his dissent from this course of action be noted in the minutes with the note that in his opinion not enough was being done to motivate the sales force and he had serious doubts concerning the effectiveness of the recently appointed sales manager. (10)

5. PERSONNEL

i) A report from the Divisional Director (Personnel) had been sent to all members and the contents were accepted. It was agreed that negotiations should commence with employee representatives to try to agree the wage increase with effect from 1 September 2001 along the lines outlined in the report.

ii) The Secretary reported that he had investigated the requirements of the current Health and Safety legislation and tabled a brief résumé of the action he felt it was necessary for the company to take in order to comply with the requirements. The Board requested him to obtain detailed cost estimates for the various requirements with, in each case, an indication of the proposed timetable for implementation of the recommendations. Action: JKL

(At this point Mr DEF apologised and, with the Chairman's permission, left the meeting.)   (11)

6. PROPERTY

The following items were noted: (12)

a) Little progress had been made on any of the pending rent reviews which would update the list accompanying the agenda for the meeting other than the following:

[Facility]: Approval was granted to a letter of response to the Landlords requesting that an extension to the user be agreed.

[Facility]: Evidence thought to be misleading had been submitted by the Landlord's agents.

[Facility]: The Landlords' agents had reduced their figure for the reviewed rent to £13,500 p.a.

b) The sale of [facility] was proceeding with exchange of contracts expected for mid-July and completion by 1 August. It was noted that receipt of the sale monies had not been built into the cash flow forecast and that if this sale completed as anticipated the additional overdraft facility would not be needed beyond the end of July.

c) The possibility of selling the business and licensing or underletting the lease at [facility] was being pursued urgently.

d) Insurance: The Secretary would draft a letter for Landlords requesting that the interest of the company be noted on the insurance policy to ensure any liability in the event of loss was minimised.   Action: JKL

7. SEALING

The Secretary produced Register of Seals to the Board and approval was granted to the affixing of the company seal to items numbered 345 to 357 and 359 to 361, and approval granted to the signing as a deed of item 358. The Chairman was authorised to sign the register in evidence of this approval.   (13)

8. BOARD MEETING TIMETABLE

The dates of the meetings of the Board for the remainder of the year were confirmed as 28 March, 26 April, 24 May, 28 June, 26 July, 30 August, 27 September, 25 October, 29 November and 20 December. The Secretary was requested to inform Messrs DEF and UVW of these dates as soon as possible.   (14)

Chairman .... 28 March 2000 (15)

Notes

1. Pages of minutes should be consecutively numbered (particularly if a loose-leaf binder is used). The subject of each minute (where applicable) should be indexed and a degree of cross-referencing provided. (The numbers for following pages have been omitted here purely in the interests of clarity.)
2. Stating the exact length of attendance of advisors, and even of members if they do not stay for the whole meeting, is advisable.
3. Not only has the apology been noted but it has been accepted. Under Table A, if a director is absent from Board Meetings for six months or more without good cause and their co-directors so decide they can be removed from office. Some companies require their directors to sign an attendance book (although it would not normally be necessary to minute this if it is done as a routine), but this is not a legal requirement.
4. See Approval and 15 below regarding the advisability of signing the minutes. Ideally the Chairman should initial each page of the minutes except for the last, which should be signed.
5. Placing the initials of the person due to deal with the item enables the minutes (already a document of record and reference) to act also as a means of encouraging action. Some companies repeat the action required with the initials and even completion dates at the end of the minutes.
6. It is important that any director with an interest in the subject matter should declare that interest and that the point be noted. Failure to do so could incur a fine of £2,000. The minutes should be referred to for the effect regarding the QUORUM of the meeting, the directors' ability to speak and/or vote on the subject, and/or the directors' rights as regards any profit made from the contract.
7. Framing a decision in this way leaves some leeway for delay should the circumstances at the time warrant such delay.
8. Where a lengthy document is required to be approved, rather than repeating the whole item in the minutes, photocopying it and attaching it to the minutes is advisable. It should then be numbered either consecutively after the last page number for that meeting, or take the number of the past page and 'a', 'b', 'c', etc., added with a designatory letter for each page of the item. Banks may wish to have a set form of resolution used.
9. Since the Articles often set out requirements and restrictions on the Board's actions, reference should be made to them.

10. In the event that any director wishes his/her dissent to be recorded this must occur although often the Chairman will seek to avoid the inclusion of such a comment since it evidences a lack of unanimity.

11. Ideally, all directors should be present for the whole meeting but if this is not possible, the time that a director left (or, if late, arrived) should be noted in the minutes.

12. To save the time of the meeting, it may be possible to distribute a report (as here) with the Agenda and simply report on any update since the date of the Agenda.

13. Although not a statutory requirement the use of a Register of seals and subsequent approval of all entries provides Board authority for the items. It also enables details to be noted of items signed as deeds where the use of the seal has been dispensed. The Chairman should sign under the last number authorised at the meeting and should add the date. Ideally the number of each seal entry in the Register should appear on the item sealed as a further cross-reference of authority.

14. When meetings are arranged in the absence of a colleague, these may clash with other commitments already entered into. Early advice of the dates is essential. Ideally the dates of Board Meetings should be arranged on a rolling 18-month basis. With the immediate six-month dates firm, the following six months subject to some leeway and the third six months indicative only. Progressively, of course, the six-month sections become firmer with additional outline indications tacked on.

15. Inserting a place for the Chairman to sign and adding the date (of the next planned meeting) emphasises the importance of signing as well as completing the audit trail.

Approval

Minutes should be prepared as soon as possible and approved in principle by the Chairman. Approval of the minutes as a true record should be sought from those present at their next following meeting. As evidence of that approval, the Chairman should initial all pages except the last, which should be signed. Usually, depending on the Articles, minutes prepared and approved in this way will stand as *prima facie* evidence of the meeting's decisions (although they may still be able to be challenged in court).

It is important that all members read the minutes and agree that they are a true record.

Case study: *Caught by own decision*

In the case of *Municipal Mutual Insurance* v *Harrop* (1998) the directors found that because a decision which they claimed they had not taken was included as a decision in minutes which they had confirmed as accurate, they were legally bound by that decision.

Negotiation

use serah

Introduction

Inherent in every meeting regardless of the constituent members and their position in their organisations is a process of negotiation. Whilst inevitably at many times there will be unanimity between the members, where this is not present then in order to more forward there will need to be some degree of compromise amongst the parties. To attain an agreed consensus the principles of negotiation (whether they are recognised as such or not) will the used. This subject is dealt with at length in the sister title to this book, *ONE STOP Negotiation,* but it may be helpful to include a résumé of the principles here.

Establish the principles

The movement of discussion in meetings depends on the principles of negotiation which include:

Checklist

1. Establish the facts in order to arrive at an initial view trying to anticipate what will be the other party's view.
2. Accept there are two sides to every story and that the other party may hold different views (even for apparently illogical reasons).
3. Research the background of the other party and endeavour to assess their likely preferred outcome and manner of approach.
4. Give weight and credence to the views of the other side. Dismissing such views out of hand is likely to provoke a negative backlash as most people want to be recognised and be proud of their contribution. This desire must be appreciated and can be played upon. Well-founded flattery, used with discretion, may be compelling (although it is possible it may be spotted for what it is).
5. Subordinate your prime preferences to achieve consensus and assess whether there is a substitute solution acceptable to both. Such 'British compromises' at least have the advantage of allowing things to progress.
6. Try to make constant movements towards the desired result,

ensuring that a flexible approach is adopted and that an entrenched position does not close off possible progress towards the ideal or substitutional end.

7. Be ready to compromise. It may not be ideal but at least it may enable progress to be made.

Tactics

In face-to-face meetings a number of tactics can be employed in order to try to ensure one's preferred outcome prevails. These can also be used in meetings where there are more numerous participants but may become diluted by the increased input.

1. Face-saving

The idea of allowing the other part to save 'face', particularly if the meeting takes place within a high-profile scenario, or on behalf of others, for example, negotiating on behalf of trade union members, is a very sound method of trying to ensure the members agree to one's original aim. Since consensus is the desired result, the instigator needs to design the conduct of the meeting to make it appear that both sides have gained something, regardless of the facts.

2. Finding the edge

This involves attempting to discover if there is a fact or any pressure which can be brought to bear on the other party to the meeting. If there is, or it is perceived that there is a hidden agenda, that is that one of the parties wishes to use the meeting for another purpose or to develop it into something different than that understood at the outset by the other, this might be used against the other player.

3. Fishing

Keeping quiet (see 13. Silence, below) tends to force other parties to speak, whereas 'fishing' involves making extreme statements to generate response and to keep the other party talking. Again the purpose is to encourage him to disclose more and more of his case, and how deeply he is committed to it.

4. Letting the other side make the running

The principle here is to allow the other party to put forward the whole of their case, even including any extra data they were hoping to hold back, before putting forward any arguments or facts oneself. This is one of the principles of interrogation: 'Let them say what they want and lead them on.' In other words, whilst someone is speaking he reveals more and more of his case and preferences, allowing the meeting instigator to hold back his ammunition for a final attack.

5. Misinformation

This involves indicating a far worse situation initially than is really required and then backtracking. For example, the statement 'I want to charge you an extra 10 per cent for the price of the goods' generates an outraged response, as a result of which the originator eventually agrees to reduce the increase to 5 per cent (which was probably the figure he had in mind in the first place). Research shows that where this is utilised the hidden (and real) alternative will gain acceptance in over 60 per cent of instances.

6. Misunderstanding

By deliberately misinterpreting the other's comments and statements, the depth of feeling on a particular subject can be revealed. This can also be used in a meeting as a ploy to ruffle the presentation of the person putting forward a case. Conversely, if it is being used against you, you need to be aware of the device and to explain the point patiently again. Indeed, it can be turned against the perpetrator with words such as: 'I am sorry you have not understood, I thought I had made it fairly clear but I'll just run through the points again.' If the instigator's aim was to put you off your stroke and draw the meeting to a swift closure, calmly running through the arguments again will be the last thing he wants as it can imply inattention on his part.

7. Non-disclosure

The principle here is to start the meeting using certain but not all relevant facts. If satisfactory progress towards the object of the encounter is not made, the use at a late stage of additional information or facts may well help the instigator to carry the day. Not using all one's ammunition at the first onslaught does enable a fresh attack to be mounted later. Conversely sometimes it may be preferable to overwhelm the opposition by means of a pre-emptive move.

8. Playing 'good guy/bad guy'

This is an example of applied psychology, where two partners in dialogue with a third person seem to be at variance with each other. The idea is that a rapport is engendered between the target and the 'good guy' who 'form an alliance' against the 'bad guy'. The aim is then to exploit the rapport thus created in the hope that the person will disclose more of his case or fall back position to his 'friend', the 'sympathetic' listener. Obviously this is more relevant for meetings for three or more persons and brings us into consideration of AMBUSHES AND ASSASSINATIONS. However, the device can be used when the 'bad guy' is not party to the meeting and the 'good guy' attempts to give the impression of forming an alliance with the other person against the 'bad guy', not present but involved in the subject matter, in order to discover more of the other person's views.

9. Power

Inevitably 'pulling rank' exerts pressure simply from the exercise of strength of position. Whilst it can work, like the exercise of pressure, it is risky and may trigger a backlash whilst being unlikely to be in the best interests of either party or the business.

10. Pre-emptive offer

One can sympathise with the logic behind this concept. If agreement can be reached on a pre-emptive offer it should certainly cut down on discussion time in the meeting. However, unless the proposal is attractive to the other party, it is risky since it negates the concept of the other party 'justifying their existence'. If the circumstances dictate using a pre-emptive offer, this should only be carried out in conjunction with a face-saver (see 1. Face-saving, above).

11. Pressure

Pressure may need to be applied in some meetings in order to achieve progress. Consensus is very acceptable, but often there are genuine and sincerely held differences of opinion. Latent pressure may consist of a swift résumé of arguments, perhaps indicating the apparent weakness of the other's case with the aim of gaining agreement, or at least acquiescence, whereas actual pressure attempts to force the issue. This, however, may put the other party on the defensive and ensure there is no resolution of the matter.

12. Rubbing salt in the wound

This reactive tactic uses as its conduit the previous activity of the other side. Most people, if they lose out in a negotiation, try to ignore the occurrence, thus applying the balm of silence to their wounded pride. However, it may be possible to use the fact that the other side gained the upper hand previously as a lever in the current negotiations.

13. Silence

When Sir Thomas More was facing imprisonment and execution for refusing to acknowledge Henry VIII as head of the Church in England he agreed to keep silent on the topic. However the very fact of his silence, in Henry's view, 'screamed up and down throughout Europe'. Silence can indicate a number of attitudes and many people cannot face it. Such people feel a pressure to fill the vacuum by speaking. In speaking, more of their case is revealed, whilst the quiet party gains ammunition for any counter-play. Silence is a particularly effective weapon in a two-party, face-to-face encounter, but it needs strong nerves to stick with it. It resembles the 'punching cotton wool' device, where in answer to a particularly annoyed or outraged other party, if the first party keeps quiet, ultimately the second party runs out of original things to say, keeps repeating themselves and ultimately dries up.

14. Sympathy and underestimation

Trying to engender sympathy for one's present position or problems may engender some rapport but, since it tends to give an impression of weakness it is unlikely to be successful. Creating in the mind of one's opponent an impression of your own apparent failings, that is an underestimation of ability, may work however. Underestimating one's opponent is a classic mistake, often causing greater disclosure of the case, believing success to be a foregone conclusion. Conversely, having created the underestimation it can be difficult then to regain a true estimation and thus to gain appropriate credence for one's views.

15. Temper

Deliberate loss of temper during a meeting in order to try to impress the other party with the level of commitment to the subject matter can be effective. However it can hardly be re-used in the same forum and, for this reason, should be used with extreme caution.

16. Threats

Although in some ways indicating the resolve with which one party views the need to agree business at a meeting, the issue of a threat can only be made once, and although bluff can carry things through, the adage 'never threaten unless you are prepared to carry the threat out' should not be overlooked. Indeed, since the prime principle of meeting work, particularly in one-to-one meetings, is to try to achieve consensus, threats should not really form part of such debate. Having said that, latent threats or hidden power, particularly if the two parties are not on the same managerial level, are present in many encounters.

Outflanking the opposition

Introduction

Meeting time is precious and even if the acid test of dividing the total salaries and oncosts of those involved in the meeting by its length to gain a cost per minute is not resorted to in order to demonstrate it, every meeting has its costs. Indeed, that time test deals only with salaries whereas there will be others, such as travel, accommodation and so on. Meetings should therefore be advertised as having a pre-set duration. This may avoid them being hijacked by destructive opposition. Whilst constructive opposition is healthy and can force reconsideration of suggestions and lead to improved decisions or solutions, some tactics are anything but constructive and must be dealt with accordingly.

The filibuster

Filibustering entails the use of speech itself as a means of delaying action. It originated as parliamentary tactics in the United States senate which, unlike the House of Representatives has no rules governing speaking duration. By means of this device, a group of senators, sometimes a sole senator as occurred in 1957 when Senator Thurmond of South Carolina talked non-stop for 24 hours, use grossly extended speeches to delay or prevent parliamentary action. The aim is to talk at such length that the majority either grants concessions or withdraws or amends the subject matter. Whilst this concept is predominantly used in the context of state legislative bodies, the filibuster can be used anywhere if time is of the essence. The onus in this situation is on the Chairman to try to ensure that the meeting is moved on to discuss the business required. Faced with a filibuster, it may be difficult the first time round to do other than accept the inevitable, but where a filibuster is anticipated, the reactions set out here may be of assistance.

Checklist

1. Implementation of a speaker's guide stating that, for example, only five minutes per speaker will be allowed on each topic, on pain of suspension from the meeting for exceeding the time limit. This could be backed up by a triple-colour light indicator. Whilst the

191

green light shows, the person can speak; when the orange light comes on, this indicates that only two minutes' speaking time is left; whilst when the red light begins to flash only 45 seconds are left. When the red light ceases flashing and remains constant the speaker must stop. Power for any microphone used can be linked so that the microphone goes dead as soon as the red light remains constant.

Example

This would normally be called 'applying the guillotine, cloture or closure' – that is cutting short the meeting by setting an overall time limit. The guillotine was first used around 1910 to ensure progress through the House of Commons of certain finance acts, but the cloture, or closure, predates it having been introduced in Parliament in 1882. It can be applied only when supported by at least 100 votes.

---

2. An announcement that should the meeting not consider all aspects of the subject matter, it will be adjourned until a set time and date. This can negate the actions of a filibuster, although if a decision is needed urgently, it may be difficult to achieve.
3. An announcement that, whether everyone has spoken or not, a decision vote on particular business will be taken at a pre-set time. Whilst ensuring progress is made, the filibuster can still be effective, as it can deny the supporters of the motion the right or opportunity to make their points.

Example

This is usually termed using a 'kangaroo' – that is cutting short discussion on a particular point by requiring a decision after a set time and hopping from that to the next business.

---

4. An announcement that only two speeches of (say) ten minutes or less will be allowed from each of the proposing and opposing sides. This rule could also be made subject to the restrictions set out in 1. above.

Loquacious members

If meetings' members are generally loquacious or garrulous they may be forced to consider making their points in a more concise manner if the meeting is held with everyone standing.

> **Example**
>
> Since the meetings of the UK Privy Council in the nineteenth century tended to take a considerable amount of time, the custom, which continues to the present day, was developed for, or at the instigation of, Queen Victoria, of holding the meetings with all participants, except presumably the Queen herself, standing. The discomfort of the position concentrated the mind on the meeting's priorities and reduced their duration!

Interestingly, some organisations in Australia use a similar idea with meeting rooms fitted with chest-high desks to facilitate note-taking but no chairs. Obviously time is not necessarily a sound criterion for a meeting's effectiveness and forcing a meeting to end swiftly when there is business requiring considered attention is as poor management of resources as convening a meeting without 'meat'.

Tangenteers

Implicit in filibustering may be a need to incorporate other subjects into the address as it will be difficult to speak for long enough on one subject to create an effective filibustering speech. Almost inevitably the filibuster will need to deviate from the main subject. This type of approach can also be used by some meeting members either to waste time, or to try to divert the attention of the meeting to a hidden agenda or pet project, or to detract attention from an item on the agenda which the member would prefer not to be discussed or to restrict discussion on such an item. Again the use of the speaker guidelines may control abuse.

Woolly wafflers

Those who, when requested to report at a meeting, seem totally incapable of marshalling thoughts, facts and recommendations into any kind of order so that a cogent report is prepared can be termed woolly wafflers: their thought processes are woolly whilst they tend to waffle. The trouble with such woolly wafflers is that often they have a grasp of the fundamentals of the subject, and indeed may have completed adequate research to enable them to assemble the required data but they simply cannot 'get it all together', or at least get it together in a way capable of assimilation by anyone other than themselves.

Time-wasters

Whilst all destructive opposition are to a greater or lesser extent time-wasters, unlike other types so far addressed, these perform their negative act not to divert attention or to ensure inadequate time be allocated to pre-set business, but simply to please themselves. Such meeting members tend to regard their presence at the meeting as a semi-social diversion, and do not seem to appreciate that the meeting has aims and results to be achieved, overriding all social aspects. Accordingly contributions from these sources tend to be somewhat divorced from reality and are usually irrelevant. The Chairman needs to bring such members back to address the business listed and may also need to address the question of whether they should remain members of the meeting at all.

Blackmailers

As meetings comprise a number of members, the opportunities for alliances are virtually unlimited. Where alliances cannot be formed there may be a temptation on the part of one or more members to try to convert the sense of the meeting to support their views by means of 'blackmail', that is by putting pressure beyond business requirements on their colleagues to agree to their pet project.

Saboteurs

Most members are committed to the interests of the meeting and the attainment of the aims of the meeting, despite at times needing to sublimate their own preferences to the long-term interests of the meeting. At times, however, the depth of feeling on particular issues can be so strong that members would apparently prefer to see the meeting collapse rather than allow it to follow a course of action.

Political manoeuvrers

This is not meant to refer to meetings held for political purposes but meetings where politicking, that is manoeuvring for personal position or advancement, takes place. Although, refreshingly, it is outlawed (at least in theory) in some organisations, nevertheless it is probably true to state that it is present to some extent in all organisations and can be particularly prevalent in large companies. The chairmen of meetings where it takes place should make every effort to try to outlaw and outmanoeuvre the manoeuvrers, or the effect will be the dilution of effort devoted to the aims of the organisation in favour of the personal aims of the individuals.

Adverse allies

Liaising with other executives has a potential downside, that is, the ally being disgraced and the taint spreading to those with whom he was associated. Conversely, remaining aloof may preserve an edge of power to the owner of the support sought after. If such support is not guaranteed but merely hinted at, contenders will be left wondering if support from such a quarter might be forthcoming. This could be a considerable help to the non-committed member in trying to manipulate support for his own preferred items of business. This kind of relationship can be termed that of the adverse ally, a person who seems ready to support and yet does not grant full commitment. Taken a step further, such a person may be ready, if not to support the other party at least not to oppose him, or further still to agree on a 'you scratch my back and I'll scratch yours' device. This may entail at least an agreement to lay off the support-seeker's territory in return for the support-seeker laying off one's own area of responsibility.

Retaining an open mind

Whilst open dissent must be controlled and channelled, some element of disagreement may be necessary if ideas are to be developed and progress made. If a meeting is becoming cosy and social rather than aloof and examining, or members regard it as an excuse for a social 'get together' rather than an examination of performance and a forum for developing plans and strategy, then the Chairman needs to manipulate the whole endeavour to ensure attention is focused on the essentials needing to be addressed by the meeting. As Shakespeare says in *Antony and Cleopatra*, 'sweet are the uses of adversity', to which we can reply 'and beneficial can be its effects in encouraging new ideas, slaughtering sacred cows and challenging established concepts'. Organisations do not stand still, as they must either progress and expand and live, or stagnate, contract and eventually die. Meetings of the bodies controlling such organisations need to be manipulated if they are not addressing the basic needs of the organisation, in the same way that members need to be manipulated in order to ensure that they do conform to the requirements of the meeting. Thus, ideally, all members should come to the meeting with an open mind, although they will almost certainly have preferences. This being the case should not prejudice them from listening to the arguments of others before arriving at a conclusion on the basis of the strength of the arguments put forward. Obviously this is an ideal and not all meetings, or all members, live up to it, or attain it at all times, as pressures may combine to influence and manipulate the member. Where this is by virtue of the force of his own commitment to the argument this may be acceptable, but where it is due to pressure from an external agency or other member it is certainly not. If the latter is suspected, then investigation should be implemented.

Presentations

Introduction

A presentation can be defined as a meeting between members with unequal roles where there is an onus on the member in control not only to lead but to generate a response and input from the other party if the encounter is to be productive. Essentially, it requires the member in control to place information before the meeting in an attempt to gain their understanding. It may approach being a dramatic performance (hence the use of dramatic headings in the following checklists) and indeed presentations which retain a sense of the dramatic may in many instances achieve an effectiveness and acceptability otherwise lacking. Unfortunately, making a presentation is thought by many to be one of the top ten most stressful experiences, which may explain why many such events are performed so poorly. Whilst most presentations may be required to be made internally, for example, to employees, senior managers and directors or their equivalent may be obliged to give presentations to bankers, prospective investors, fund managers, etc. A poor performance to employees may involve little downside (even though it may impair the reputation of the manager involved) – however, a poor presentation to external contacts could have a potentially damaging effect on the reputation of both director and company. Thus many of the principles in the following section will be the same although the informality suggested for employees may be out of place in such instances.

Background

To ensure a presentation is successful, those who are required to present need to receive guidance in how to manage the challenge. They should be reassured to some extent since in many instances the audience may be as nervous as they are. To those employees not used to such meetings, etc., simply attending a formal briefing or presentation may be regarded as an inhibiting and ego-questioning experience. The problem then is that they are unlikely to respond even to the most earnest entreaties to participate. However experience indicates that the more informal and relaxed such a meeting is, the more likely there is to be employee feedback and input. This should give the presenter a clue to their own challenge:

- to make it informal;
- to relax those present to encourage feedback and retention;
- to prepare the messages required to be presented in a way that the audience can understand;
- to use visual aids to help receptivity;
- to provide notes to aid recall;
- to keep the tone light-hearted without being flippant;

and so on.

Checklist – The staging

Presentation commitment and guidelines
1. The [organisation] wishes line and other managers to give regular BRIEFINGS to their employees in order to keep them advised regarding developments, provide lines of communication for matters of concern to employees and a means by which both parties can understand the other.
2. Such briefings should be regarded as an essential part of the management, leadership and motivation of the workforce and, in order to generate a genuine two-way flow of comment, etc. need to be set up and conducted in as informal a way as possible.
3. Presentational briefings, whatever the subject, will only be effective if:
    a) the briefer is totally in command of their subject (to achieve which they must ensure they prepare adequately);
    b) the briefer gives attention to the structure of the encounter itself; and
    c) the following guidelines are observed.

Guidelines
1. Stand in a relaxed manner. In this way it is physically easy to speak and you will command attention – it is also easier to breathe deeply if you are nervous.
2. Speak without a jacket (if male) informally dressed (if female). Whilst in some instances this may be inappropriate, normally it will indicate to those present that you mean business, whilst the perceived informality may help them (and you) relax.
3. Make eye contact with the audience. Whilst this can be difficult with more than, say, 40 participants, eye contact creates rapport and enables the speaker to check receptivity. If the speaker can

see that eyes are becoming glazed or puzzled (s)he may be able to recap and attempt to make the point more clearly, whilst if they become closed, an attention gainer may be needed.

4. The room should be arranged informally – as unlike a classroom as possible. Curved or horseshoe-like layouts are preferable to straight rows. If straight lines are unavoidable setting them in a herring-bone design may break up the classroom image. In addition the herring-bone arrangement has the advantage of focusing the attention on a single central point – the position where the speaker should stand. Ideally no person should be more than 25 feet from the speaker.

5. Unless the briefer knows forenames of all those present those attending should be asked to write their forenames on nameplates to be placed in front of them. If an employee poses a question, the briefer should then be able to use the name to personalise the interface and to aid the creation of rapport and informality.

6. Humour should be used – but only with discretion. Making participants laugh both relaxes them and makes delegates inhale oxygen which (at least in theory) restores their attention and offsets drowsiness. Conversely, too much laughter may belittle the presentation. However, since learning tends to be most effective when the subject is relaxed and humour aids relaxation, this can assist. Humour may also ease tension in those who find the encounter frightening. Ideally, the humour should be spontaneous and arise naturally from the presentation, rather than being rehearsed. Thus humorous comments developed from the actual session, rather than jokes, are preferable.

7. Avoid distractions, both personal and within the room. Windows should be masked if they open onto an area which can provide distractions. The briefing room should not have a telephone, whilst visitors and interruptions, as well as any extraneous noise, should be avoided.

8. The room should neither be too hot nor too cold. Smoking should not be allowed – it is a distraction and an annoyance to non-smokers. Water and/or juice should be provided – particularly for the speaker as both nerves and constant speaking can dry the mouth.

9. The briefer should be able to see all those present and the audience should be able to see him/her. Notes should be provided so that employees do not have to spend time writing these and are only required to write their own amplifying comments – if needed. (Whilst making notes may help delegates retain the

subject matter the problem for many is that their attention to the notetaking detracts from what is then being said.)

10. Simplicity should be the watchword, with jargon avoided or at least explained. The notes should be prepared and arranged in order of presentation so that everything proceeds smoothly. Nothing causes embarrassment or disruption more than the briefer being unable to find their place. Similarly all aids and handouts should also be arranged in order.

11. With smaller groups, distributing handouts of particular importance during the session can aid rapport between briefer and employees. It should also assist the break up of any formality of the session as well as concentrating the attention on the particular item. Movement (even the simple act of passing a piece of paper to one's neighbour) attracts attention – and reawakens interest.

12. Logical progression of content is essential, with appropriate links between subjects. If the order of content is unrelated, employees may become confused, and if they are confused their attention will wander. Ease of familiarity with the subject matter is all-important.

13. Using visual aids will complement the briefing, add interest and encourage attentiveness. All equipment (computer display, video, slide projector, overhead projector, and so on) should be checked and alternatives made available so that if there is a failure the disruption can be minimised. If all else fails there should always be a flip chart. Don't overuse the equipment however – it should add interest and complement the verbal content and dialogue without overwhelming it.

14. Questions and comments should be encouraged. Again this will aid rapport and enable the briefer to check that the points have been taken on board by those present. Questions should be answered as honestly as possible and if asked a question to which the answer is not known, the briefer should say so and promise to get back to the questioner having checked the point out.

15. Take questions during the presentation not at the end. This will encourage employees to regard the briefing as more of a conversation and less of a formal meeting.

16. In larger groups, recognise that many delegates will be inhibited from posing questions verbally – either through a fear of speaking publicly or through a fear that the question will be regarded as 'silly'. In these circumstances, encourage the use of written questions, providing pads for the purpose.

17. At the outset stress the invitation to join in and if it is likely that

questions may be slow to originate, arrange with some delegates to ask predetermined questions.

18. Before the presentation rehearse roughly what you wish to say by speaking aloud whilst looking into a mirror. This will not only allow you to hear what the words will sound like to the audience but may also allow you to spot if you have any mannerisms of which you are not aware but which could be distracting to the audience. Listening to or watching a tape-recording or video of the rehearsal could also be valuable although care should be taken not to be too self-critical – after all the audience will only see the presentation once and will not have the benefit of a replay button to analyse mistakes. Indeed most mistakes will go completely unnoticed – as is the case even in professional theatre performances.

19. A presentation is a performance – treat it like one. Making a presentation is akin to playing a role on the stage – the speaker needs to be:
    - a little larger than life;
    - word-perfect if possible (notes can be referred to but should *never* be read); and
    - able at all times to make the subject matter interesting.

Case study:	*Attention required*

1. Attention grabbers – intended
   One of the subjects on which I give seminars is 'How to write an effective report' for, among others, employees involved in administering payrolls. In searching for a way of making the subject memorable I decided to fire a starting pistol at the commencement of the presentation, asking delegates to describe the loud noise that they heard. Usually after a little prompting the fact that it was a 'gun's report 'was mentioned. Delegates were then asked to describe the sound and fairly easily the descriptions 'short, sharp and provoke attention' surfaced and were written one under the other in a flip chart. Asking them which department they worked for and ringing the initial letters SSP generated the question of whether the letters meant anything to them. Obviously working in payroll departments they

recognised the initials of Statutory Sick Pay, but were then told that in future the letters stood for Short Sharp and Provoke attention which were the essential characteristics of a good report as demonstrated by the gun's report. Checking retention of subject matter two years later indicated that only a tiny percentage could not remember what the new mnemonic of SSP stood for.

2. Attention grabbers – unintended (and unwanted)

a) The Chairman was used to commanding attention and experienced in chairing Board Meetings. He was not, however, used to speaking to a number of people within a more formal context. At a conference, at which he had to give the keynote presentation, he was very nervous. This nervousness manifested itself in a habit of keeping his left hand in his trouser pocket constantly fingering a set of keys. The sound of these keys jingling was such a distraction to the audience that the impact of his words was lost. During coffee break the discussion was more about the Chairman's keys than his words!

b) The manager was similarly unused to speaking and was equally nervous. Although he had prepared his presentation he had not delivered it out loud. The first time he heard it was when he was standing in front of the delegates. His favourite word was 'obviously', which unfortunately he kept repeating so much so that the delegates noticed the repetition and several started keeping a note of the number of 'obviouslys'. So widespread did this become that it seriously impaired the effectiveness of his presentation – the delegates were more interested in the word than the theme.

The challenge

Apart from keeping the delegates awake and interested, which is an ongoing challenge, we have communication barriers with which to contend. Research indicates that of what people read they will retain around 10 per cent, of what they hear they will retain 20 per cent, but that when they both see and hear (as they do during a presentation) they will retain around 50 per cent and thus this means of communication is more effective than many others. Further, if feedback and questions from the audience are encouraged and take place during the presentation (which is necessary if it is to be most effective) then retention of subject matter may rise to around 70 per cent – a similar retention level as that for a conversation.

Visual aids

It is probably no exaggeration to state that all presentations can be improved by the use of visual aids. Good aids well used can both illustrate and enliven the talk. However, they need to be linked with the content, well-prepared and handled with care. These aids should enhance and extend a presentation and in addition:

- they save time, since a picture can be worth a thousand words and an easily emphasise a message or create a theme with ease;
- the visual image can be a powerful aid to memory retention;
- a slide can clarify an idea more easily than words (although it is important to check that this is the effect – some slides can actually confuse rather than elucidate).

Checklist – Scenery

Video
These should only be used if the session is long (e.g. four hours or more) otherwise the video may overshadow the rest of the presentation.
Powerpoint
These work by computer-generated material being projected on to a screen. The critical factor is to make sure the computer works. Too many presenters have been let down by these systems at the last minute and then have no back-up.
35 mm slides
Again there is reliance on a mechanical aid which experience indicates can fail.

> **Note**
>
> A shared problem of all three is that although they can be effective, they require no movement on the part of the presenter.

Overhead projector
The generation of these slides is easy – even hand-drawn transparencies can be effective. The trick is:
- not to put too much on them;
- to use large size letters;
- to make sure the machine is clean and in fully working order.

Flip charts
Presenters should always have a flip chart (or white board) available – then if all else fails there is a back-up. Research indicates that delegates tend to remember best:
a) what they have contributed; and
b) what they have seen written in front of them (i.e. rather than on prepared material).
When using a flip chart:
- write clearly and straight
- check spelling of any words that might be generated
- use a small crib if you could forget copy (i.e. any item is written lightly in pencil on a flip chart, cannot be seen by delegates and can thus act as a crib for presenter).

Warning

 A white board is not the same as a flip chart – it does not allow the presenter to return to 'previous pages' as to use more space what is already inscribed needs to be removed. Whilst the surface is far superior, this lack of flexibility can be a serious drawback for presentations of any length.

Tricks of the trade

A presenter needs to give a performance but only if the act itself contains attractions will the attention of the delegates be retained until the conclusion.

Checklist – Rehearsals

1. **Attention grabber**. The audience needs to have its attention retained at all times. During the presentation it may be necessary to introduce deliberate attention grabbers. Responsibility for retaining attention rests with the presenter.
2. **Repetition**. An old training adage runs 'You need to tell 'em you're going to tell 'em, tell 'em, and tell 'em that you've told 'em'! Basically, we all need a certain amount of repetition in order to retain the messages we are trying to learn.
3. **Stimulation**. Attention is more likely to be retained if we can introduce gimmicks that stimulate the audience. 'Presenting at' people whereby all they are required to do is to listen may be necessary in a few instances but generally more will be achieved if speakers try to generate audience participation. Asking for input and questions keeps the audience's attention stimulated – basically because to ask a question we have to engage our brain.
4. **Relate theory to practice**. Lecturing on theory may be necessary but most people need to see how this relates to real life. True anecdotes (real-life experiences) help satisfy this need. If some of the anecdotes show the speaker making a mistake *and* learning from it, again this aids rapport. Anecdotes which only show the speaker in a good light may irritate and alienate the audience.
5. **Timing**. It may be safer to produce more material (i.e. in notes and slides) than is necessary on the basis that you are then very unlikely to 'run out'. You can usually cut excess material down – it is very rare that you can invent new material on the spot if you find you are running short.
6. **Arrive in time**. Presenters should always leave time to sort themselves out, arrange everything the way they want it, check the machinery and the layout, and still have time for 15 minutes to have a drink quietly and compose themselves. Arriving in a rush just before commencement, without time to sort papers and other matters out, etc., can lead to a poor presentation. It hardly sends the appropriate message to the delegates.
7. **Modulate your voice**. Monotones are monotonous. Monotony will lose you your audience so mix your presentation up – using aids (visual and written) to break the voice – and vary its pitch.
8. **Make eye contact**. Keep looking at and meeting the eyes of your audience – it helps build links (rapport) between speaker and listener. It also helps the speaker to check that the eyes (and therefore the brains) of the audience are still switched on to him or her.

9. **Pauses** —— can be effective. They can help the audience recap on what has been said, help the speaker take a drink or a breather, and concentrate attention – the break from the sound of the voice can also cause any in the audience who have 'drifted off' to regain attention.

10. **Question slips** can be used to encourage those who are too shy to actually speak up and ask a question.

11. **Humour**. This needs to be handled very carefully and the best advice may be not to try it. Humour that develops from the presentation naturally is the best kind. Raising a laugh from the audience can be very helpful since the act of laughing draws oxygen into the body, which helps regain attention. A greater amount of oxygen being present means the listener is unlikely to drift off to sleep!

12. **Practise, practise, practise**. Only if you practise – in front of a mirror, to a tape-recorder (to check what it sounds like), to a camcorder (to check what it looks and sounds like) – will you gain confidence.

Beating the nerves

Confidence is contagious – but so is a lack of it. The presenter needs to have confidence and this can only be evinced if there has been adequate preparation.

Checklist – Learning the lines

1. Be prepared – know your subject, practice your presentation.
2. Look at the audience as if you were having a conversation with each one.
3. Wear clothes in which you are comfortable.
4. Arrive in plenty of time – get your breath back and organise the room so you are happy with it.
5. Highlight the key words or points of your notes so they act as guide, prompt and support.
6. Go off with a bang! – ideally something original that will grab attention.
7. Learn the first few minutes of the session word perfect. Once you have started you will feel much better.
8. Remember the old advice about giving a speech – imagine you are drilling – if you haven't struck oil in the first three minutes – stop boring!
9. NEVER, NEVER, NEVER start with an apology (e.g. 'I'm not very

good at this but...') – it will immediately denigrate you in the perception of the audience – and destroy their confidence in you as a presenter. Start with confidence and the audience will appreciate this. First impressions are very important and you only have once chance.

10. A presentation is a performance and like an actor playing his part on stage your performance needs to be a little larger than life.

11. Speak up so that everyone can hear (although speaking softly on occasion can also gain attention – and so can pauses).

12. Invite the audience to join in, ask questions, make comments, provide feedback. Not only will they remember the session more accurately, they will also feel part of it – and probably rate it more highly.

13. To try to get the audience prepared to ask questions. Say, 'Good morning'. Delegates will almost inevitably reply so that is the first time of speaking. This should make it easier for some delegates to talk again.

14. Ask straightforward, uncontroversial questions at the start. This may gain response and once one or two people speak up others will follow. (Be careful, though: there will always be some who never speak.)

15. If you think it may be difficult to gain a response then prime one person with pre-arranged comments or questions. Once (s)he has spoken the others may feel less inhibited.

16. Be enthusiastic. Enthusiasm is infectious and most people warm to it. A ready smile will win over all but the harshest of critics.

17. The overwhelming majority of delegates want the speaker to do well – they are on your side!

18. Presentations must have purpose and point. Ensure the purpose and point is identified with the organising body (and in writing) and then research the purpose(s) accordingly.

19. Check and recheck that your presentation addresses the purpose required – and that it is in a logical order/sequence.

20. It may help to summarise at the beginning what you are going to do – and then at the end what you have done. Hopefully these will coincide – and if they do not rewrite the presentation!

The hardware

As well as the person, a presenter needs certain hardware to hand to ensure that the presentation goes smoothly.

Checklist – Props

 A presenter needs to be prepared for all eventualities and may need:

- a cleaner for the overhead projector (some screens are never covered when not in use);
- pens for the flip chart;
- OHP pens if you want to write on slides;
- nameplates in case there are none;
- a penknife and/or scissors in case you need to cut open parcels, make nameplates, etc.;
- 'bluetack' in case you want to display items;
- spare sheets of paper in case you want to cover slides;
- a clock (never look at your watch!);
- a rest for your notes (it is easier to look at something propped up than papers lying flat);
- a glass of water (talking continuously can make you dry);
- a pointer;
- throat and headache tablets;

and so on.

Note

To repeat the actor's warning of the last thing to do before going on stage – check your zip (or buttons).

Quorum

Introduction

'Quorum' is Latin for 'of whom' and has come colloquially to be the indicator for the minimum number of persons present in order that a meeting or body can legally conduct business. If that minimum number is not present then the meeting is said to be 'inquorate' and business attempted to be conducted thereat is invalid although presumably any decisions taken could be subsequently ratified by a quorate meeting although this is would be an potentially unreliable and unsatisfactory base to argue that such decisions should be taken (i.e. simply in the expectation of subsequent ratification).

General Meetings

The rules regarding the legality of meetings of the shareholders will be set out in the company's Articles of Association and these may state a minimum number of shareholders need to be present for business to be transacted. Thus Table A (Article 40) stipulates that no business can be transacted at a meeting unless there are present two members either in person or by proxy or by authorised representative. If there is no quorum present then after 30 minutes the meeting will be adjourned to the same day of the week following and at the same time and place (Article 41). Obviously these rules only apply to companies that have adopted Table A as their Articles and thus individual companies may require a higher level of quorum (e.g. 10 per cent of the voting share capital).

Of course, care needs to be taken that a meeting does not become inquorate during its term – for example, if the quorum is three shareholders and there are three present at the start of the meeting the meeting is quorate. If, however, one shareholder leaves prior to the conclusion of the meeting, the meeting then becomes inquorate from the point the shareholder left and should cease to conduct business.

Board Meetings

Table A (Article 89) stipulates that the directors may fix their own quorum and if they fail to do so then the quorum will be two. An alternate director can be counted as part of the quorum if his/her principal is not present.

Subject to the wording of individual company Articles, difficulties may arise with directors who have interests in third parties. Very often Articles will state that a director who is an interested party may not vote or take part in the discussion of the business relating to that party. However, some Articles take the prohibition further and state that a director with an interest will not be counted in the quorum for the meeting when discussing the matter which is the subject of his interest (Article 95 in Table A). This would mean that a Board Meeting could be quorate for all matters except that in which the director had an interest. One way round this (provided it is allowed for in the Articles) would be for all the directors to sign the resolution. This avoids the need to call a meeting and to obtain a quorum.

Evidencing the meeting's quorate status

To ensure that it can be proved that a quorum was present to transact the business of the meeting, the names of those present should be stated in the minutes of the meeting. Some companies also require those present to sign an attendance book. Leaving before the end of a meeting should be discouraged, but in the event of a member arriving after the start or leaving prior to the end this should be noted in the minutes.

Report writing

Introduction

Reports must rank as one of the more widely used methods of conveying information and formulating documents of record – particularly in order to brief meetings of Board or executive committees. Unfortunately, often the basic principles regarding report writing tend to be overlooked which is very regrettable since as well as being a document of (dated) record, a well-written report can act as both information provider and discussion generator.

Basic requirements

The prime purpose of a report is to provide information to the target audience. Thus the first considerations must be to determine:

a) the information that is to be provided; and
b) the target audience.

Normally a report will be commissioned in terms such as:

'The likely effect of the proposed introduction of the new procedure for X',

or

'Consider the incidence of absenteeism in the organisation and its ancillary costs, and make recommendations regarding methods of reducing both'.

The commissioning sentence may be sufficient to delineate the scope of the report but if not clarification should be obtained before work commences.

Once the purpose of the report is clear, this requirement should be written in large letters very clearly at the commencement of the draft report so that each time the report is worked on its purpose is in front of the author as a reminder. Experience indicates many reports fail to keep to the subject requested and thus fail to answer the questions posed.

Basic considerations

1. Purpose
    All reports are commissioned for a purpose – for example, to allow the

Board to take a decision. In such a case the target audience is clear and the author should ensure the report is written with the requirements of (in this case) the Board always in mind.

2. Define the target audience and present the report with their requirements in mind

    If the report is for the Board, few will relish a bulky report no matter how accurate the content. Thus if writing for such an audience the author would be advised to keep the report:
    *   short and
    *   sharp, to
    *   provoke the attention of the reader

    (ensuring that at all times it keeps to the question posed).

3. Recommendations

    If the terms of reference require recommendations to be made, these must be made and substantiated by the data and research included.

4. The permanence of print

    A printed report is a permanent record of work and views and is also a permanent reflection of the author. A report that is verbose, rambles and misses the point reflects badly on the author.

5. Language

    The language of the report must be that which is acceptable to the target audience. Normally ordinary everyday English should be used as then there should then be little chance of misunderstanding. Jargon should be avoided unless either:

    a) it is certain that all members of the target audience will understand; or

    b) a glossary explaining the jargon is incorporated in the report.

6. Timing

    Often the report will be required to be prepared by a certain date. A report which misses the date required (other than for exceptional reasons) will again not reflect well on the author.

Layout

Experience indicates that some report authors seem unable to realise that a report needs cohesion and logical progression – literally a logical beginning, middle and end. For those not experienced at writing reports it may also be helpful to generate a layout sheet indicating at least initial ideas for what information will be placed where within the report.

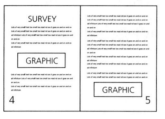

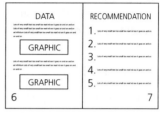

The 'beginning' section could include the title of the report (which if carefully worded can give an instant guide to the subject matter), the author and date (which will fix the recommendations at a certain time) and the question, aims or terms of reference of the report possibly with an outline of the recommendations immediately adjacent thereto.

Note

The value of this is that if the question originally posed is immediately followed by the answer(s) suggested, it should:

a) enable the author to check that the question has actually been answered;

b) aid readers who are short of time, as simply reading this page should give them an instant view of the purpose and conclusions of the report;

c) condition the recipients to the stance taken in the production of the report – with which as they study the content they can either agree or disagree.

The 'middle' section of the report should include details of the research carried out and the data generated which will prompt the conclusions or recommendations. In this area there may be a great temptation to recite all the research particularly if this is substantial. However, the reason for doing this needs to be carefully examined and the question 'Am I doing this because the target audience needs to see the research or is it that having carried out all this work I am determined someone should see how methodical/how much time I have spent on this/how diligent I have been in the preparation of this report?' needs to be answered. Generally, the recital of full data rather than a synopsis of the salient points may not add to the report and can detract from its effectiveness since the reader's attention may decline in direct proportion to increased length.

In the 'end' section will be the conclusion, recommendations, etc. Since often the author of a report may not be present when the target audience reads it, it may be helpful not only to repeat here the outline recommendations that may have already been included in the 'beginning' section, but to supplement these with explanations which may enable the author to pre-empt the questions that may form in the mind of the reader.

Presentation

A poor report can be made to appear at least reasonable by careful presentation, but a good report can be all but destroyed by poor presentation. This is not to say that presentation is everything but there is no doubt that, living in a visually orientated society, how an item is presented can 'say' a great deal about it before a word is written.

Checklist

1. Any piece of written material needs to seize the attention of the target audience, and then retain such attention throughout its length. The opening paragraph will set the scene for the rest of the content and it is vital that this paragraph is effective and 'attention-seizing'.

2. In these days of computer printers that are able to cram over 100 characters on a line of type, the valuable 2.5 alphabet rule seems to have been overlooked. This rule states that no line of type should contain more than 65 characters (counting as a character every letter and punctuation mark). The reason for the rule is simple: if a paragraph of more than 6–7 lines is printed with over this number of characters then, without a straight edge under the line, the human eye may find it difficult to retain register on the 4th or 5th or later lines and can wander to the lines above or below. (As an example, a full line of type in this book contains on average around 62 characters.)

3. Inserting headings and subheadings, paragraph key words, or even bold type, can also aid the reader finding their way to its salient points.

4. Using short but varied length paragraphs (say between 130 and 200 words) may retain the average reader's attention whereas using long and densely presented paragraphs may not.

5. The controlled use of graphics can also aid the effectiveness of a report. Literally, since one picture can be worth 1,000 words, using pie charts, bar charts and graphs can provide an instant impression of the salient points of a mass of statistics and proportions which would otherwise take the reader some time to assimilate. Any suggestion that using graphics in place of tables of statistics is somehow patronising should be resisted – all that is being attempted is to make it as easy (and as quick) as possible for the reader to assimilate the information.

6. If the report is to be printed on both sides of the page (so that page 2 appears on the back of page 1, and so on) the 'odd' (right-hand) pages will normally capture more attention than the 'even' (left-hand) pages. In addition, when faced with a double page the human eye comes initially to rest about a third the way down the odd (right-hand) page. Hence placing information in such a position should ensure it gains attention. To ensure the eye is directed elsewhere headings, graphics – even items in boxes (which invariably capture attention) need to be used.

7. Most reports are presented to their audience as pages clipped together with a staple. However the simple addition of two sheets as covers (let alone anything more sophisticated), can add a great deal to the report's initial perception. Presented in this way the report gains an impression of quality – and reflects as such on the author.

Language

Whilst the way the report appears to the target audience is important, the content is obviously its most important factor. The author needs to ensure that the language is clear and unambiguous (as well as appropriate to the target audience). It may be safest to avoid jargon and use ordinary every-day English. However we need to ensure that the words used are interesting. Repeated use of the same verb for example can make the content uninspired and the language boring.

In speech – and particularly in discussions during meetings – we do not always construct proper sentences. Indeed very often we do not finish a sentence, or interrupt ourselves, or go off at a tangent to our original intent. Whilst this may be acceptable in (non-permanent) speech, this approach cannot be used in written communication. We need to be careful with sentence and paragraph construction – ideally keeping to simple sentences and paragraphs containing only one idea. Whilst the occasional complex sentence may be acceptable, we should certainly avoid tapeworm sentences.

Example

'Tapeworm sentences comprise complex, and, very often, long, sentences, with little bits, only loosely connected, which are intended, although they usually fail, to form one long, and usually rambling, sentence, that finishes up in a format, often very complicated, which ensures that by the time the reader, if he or she perseveres, reaches the end, they have probably forgotten the point, if there ever was one.'

[*This is a tapeworm sentence.*]

Revision

Very few of us can draft a report in its final form from scratch. Ideally, a report should be generated over a period of time allowing for rewrites and revisions of drafts so that it is finely tuned and polished – using the word processor to cope with the valuable second and third thoughts.

SARAH

negotiation p185

p20 communications

> **Introduction**
>
> The best meetings may well be those that have a personal interface. Even meetings where the participants are not physically adjacent, provided there are audiovisual links, being able to see the face and attitude of the other party should aid effectiveness. This is far more difficult with meetings over the phone or by other electronic means. Effectiveness of interfacing may depend as much on the attitude, demeanour and disposition of the meeting members as on the resolution of subject matter. Indeed, in meetings where the interests of the participants may not be entirely aligned, the way in which one member operates may condition the attitude and reaction of the other to such an extent that either success or failure results. Adopting the principles of SARAH may assist. Whilst these principles should hold good in all interfacing, they may be particularly useful if the meeting is convened to convey BAD NEWS, etc.

Background

Anyone seeking to learn attitudes and everyone who has to interface with people may need guidance and assistance to ensure they can perform this essential task well. It is probably true that the best communicators and leaders are born, but all of us can improve – and if our aim is to be good at communicating and getting what we want from meetings, it is vital that we do. The principles of good direct communication and interfacing can be summed up in the process described by the mnemonic SARAH. SARAH originated in the USA and was intended originally for use more in selling, but the principles apply equally to relationships in general and to meeting transactions in particular:

- Smile and Stop talking
- Active listening
- Repeat or Reflect content
- Act with empathy and
- Handle the subject matter with appreciation of the other party's feelings.

Smile and/or Stop talking

Whenever one party is talking the other cannot be heard and neither can their views, suggestions or concerns. Nothing riles people more than for the other party to keep talking, preventing them putting their point. It often then appears to them that an attempt is being made to 'talk out' the subject matter which can only damage rapport and encourage antipathy. Conversely, smiling (particularly of a superior) relaxes most people and may encourage them to 'open up'. Smiling can also convey latent messages:

Case study: *Smile – they're watching*

As a little bit of fun for inclusion in the company newspaper at Christmas, the editor invited employees to send in their favourite memories of the year. Out of twenty or so that were received, three referred to 'the Managing Director's smile'. The editor was intrigued and in conversation with one of those who had mentioned this brought the chat round to the Managing Director. He discovered that when they saw the M.D. smile, the staff felt that everything was fine and felt that they could talk to him – but when he was not smiling, they kept out of his way as 'things' were obviously not going so well.

Key technique:

This is another example of the hidden messages communicated by body language. No doubt often when he was not smiling, the M.D. may have been preoccupied with other matters – not even necessarily work-related, but the impression in a small tightly knit company was that unless the M.D. was smiling the staff felt they could not approach him. In such circumstances, communication and motivation cannot take place. In view of the small numbers involved one would expect communication where few people are employed to be most effective, but MORI found in a recent survey that organisations employing fewer than 100 people were actually the least effective communicators.

Active listening

The corollary to ceasing to talk is to listen more – which itself will be encouraged by a smile. This means much more than hearing what is said as indicated earlier. Hearing is purely a mechanical act, whereas listening entails active consideration of what is both said and left unsaid bearing in mind that the speaker may be saying what he or she thinks the other party (particularly their manager) wants to hear. Only if we listen constantly will we gain the real views of the other party. The more we talk the more we reveal of our true feelings. In addition the longer the other party is allowed to talk and believe that the discussion will achieve some results, the greater should be their commitment. Most people want to be involved and to feel that their views count and can assist – this is particularly true of employees, nearly 50 per cent of whom complain that they are not involved enough even though they would like to be.

Repetition of content

In order to show that one party has understood what the other has said they should repeat key sentences or comments in their own words. This has four advantages:

- it helps fix the details of any problem, or the other party's views, in the mind of the recipient;
- it helps check that what has been received was what was meant by the other party;
- it engenders a rapport and understanding between the two which should lead to greater commitment and motivation; and
- it leads to really accurate communication.

Case study: *Irritation breeds discontent*

One of the responsibilities of the new production manager was to interface with the union representatives. Previously industrial relations had been very harmonious and a spirit of 'constructive compromise' had usually overcome difficulties. Within a short space of time this disintegrated and the Personnel Director investigated. She found that in place of the previous rapport between manager and chief shop steward, there was now considerable enmity. Sitting in on a routine discussion, she realised that the shop steward was inarticulate and found it difficult to express himself. Whereas his predecessor had possessed the patience to assist the steward to put his feelings into the appropriate words, the present manager had no such patience and was dismissive of the steward's stumbling attempts to express himself.

> **Key technique:**
>
> Many employees suffer from this problem. The onus, in the interest of good communication and motivation, is then on the management to assist. Ignoring or, far worse, ridiculing the problem serves merely to aggravate and destroy rapport. It may seek to enhance the status of the respondent, but this is likely to be a cheap and short-lived victory.

Act with empathy

This entails one party demonstrating clearly that they understand and appreciate the feelings and motivation of the other and is particularly important when managers are dealing with employees in BAD NEWS and DISCIPLINARY, etc., meetings. If empathy and perception are lacking, employees will conclude that they are wasting their time as the organisation does not really care about their views. Conversely, if management is seen to have listened and then to have acted, even if only partially, in the way required by the employee, again commitment and motivation is likely to be achieved.

Handle the subject matter with appreciation of the other party's feelings

One of the most widespread failings is the attitude that can be called 'corporate arrogance' – the belief that everything the organisation does is correct and that:

a)   no one else's views are worth listening to;
b)   every view not in accordance with the corporate view is not worth listening to; and
c)   everyone is subservient to the corporate view and must immediately comply with its every demand.

This is a foolish and short-sighted (albeit widespread) attitude, the effect of which can seldom be other than creating resentment, animosity, antagonism. The guide in meeting discussions, NEGOTIATIONS, and so on, is to try to put oneself in the shoes of the other person and imagine how one would feel if the positions were reversed.

In dealing with employees it is vital to appreciate that the concerns of most employees revolve around their position and security. In a recent survey by Cranfield School of Management concerning employee ideal requirements from their employment 'security' was placed second only to 'an interesting and enjoyable job'.

Secretary and meeting administration

Introduction

In many ways the role of the Secretary of a meeting is key to its success since if he has not and does not provide the administrative back up to the meeting members, their effectiveness and productivity can be severely impaired. In terms of limited liability companies, senior figures including Chairmen of the largest companies have rated the appointment of the Company Secretary as more important than that of many directors. For other meetings the profile of the Secretary may be much lower but nevertheless the administrative role undertaken and not least the generation of the record of the decisions taken is all important.

Board Meetings

The responsibility of the Secretary before and at Board Meetings entails a variety of requirements customised in accordance with the particular entity. However, in general these duties comprise:

Checklist

1. Generate an agenda in liaison with the chairman. Depending on the particular organisation the Agenda should be derived from:
   a) a timetable
   b) items from an earlier meeting
   c) new business
   d) items requested by members
   (Note
   Such additions may require the Chairman's prior approval.)
   e) regular control reports
   f) market, economic or legal changes
   g) statutorily (or similar) required items

2. Convene the meeting in due time. Meetings are usually convened by sending out the Agenda with details of the time and place of the meeting. The Agenda should be despatched at least seven days prior to the meeting, following a set format and order. Grouping like items may assist the logical 'flow' of the business. All members must be sent an Agenda as they have an obligation to attend.

3. Ensure, if a quorum (see below) is required to be present before the meeting can commence, that at least members satisfying that requirement are to be present to avoid wasting the time of others attending.

4. Take, report and record any apologies for absence (see below).

5. Check members have all the documents required.

6. Have available spare documents in case members have mislaid or forgotten them.

7. Ensure meeting's supports, refreshments, note-taking aids, protection against interruption, and so on, are present. The room needs to be large enough that meeting members do not feel inhibited by being cramped. It should also be effectively temperature-controlled so that members feel neither too hot nor too cold. There should be sufficient seats for all (allowing for visitors who may only be staying for a short part of the meeting) and such seating should be reasonably comfortable. Some members may like to be able to illustrate their ideas and views and thus having a flip chart or white board available may help. If a clock is in the room it may help focus attention on concluding the meeting within a reasonable time.

8. Ensure meeting adheres to and does not overlook any item on the agenda.

9. Ensure those who speak and vote are entitled to do so.

10. Ensure meeting's decisions are clear and clearly understood by all present.

11. Note the sense of the meeting in the minutes and query what is required with the Chairman if this is unclear.

12. Support the Chairman throughout including warning him in advance if he becomes aware of any members' concerns, etc.

13. Keep the minutes secure and available to members.

14. Ensure action is effected as required by the meeting and reported on at the appropriate time.

Administration

The Secretary is responsible for the administration of the meeting and the various items covered under this general heading are set out below.

1. Surroundings

The surroundings or location of a meeting can play an important part in determining the type and length of the meeting. If the room is formal and austere, then members may be conditioned to make their contributions short and precise, and it is likely that a greater degree of concentration on the subject in hand will be generated. Conversely, if the room is comfortable and relaxed, so too may be the deliberations, and the meeting may lose edge, competitiveness and commercialism.

Case study: *Comfort detracts from decision-making*

The company had grown rapidly, but the custom of holding Board Meetings in the lounge of the founder's house had persisted. However, the fact that members sat in armchairs in a very comfortable lounge almost inevitably led to a more chatty than businesslike attitude to the meeting. In addition the fact that the owner, the Chairman, was also in fact, if not in intent, playing host, militated against objective consideration of some of his pet plans. Finally, the fact that the Board were meeting in a house rather than an office inevitably led to them taking longer than they would otherwise have taken over the discussion of the business.

Key technique:

The effects on the meeting of its physical surroundings must not be underestimated. When the meetings were moved to the company's offices the Board lost some of its informality, and only lasted half as long. The move also had an effect on the rest of the company, which tended to relax when the Board met in the owner's house, as it was five miles distant, but were kept more alert when it met in the office.

If a particular meeting is likely to be contentious, then it may be better for it to be held in 'neutral' territory rather than in the home base of one or other of the main protagonists. Using one person's home base, that is their own office, to stage the meeting, gives that person an exploitable advantage.

2. Composition

The meeting should be restricted to those who have a right to be present – with no supernumeraries. If the number of participants is swollen by those who either have no purpose being there or whose contribution is minimal or useless, then the effectiveness of the other members as well as the meeting itself will be impaired. Restricting membership in this way may need to be qualified with some 'review of business meetings' where the progress of several disciplines is to be considered. Even in this scenario, however, attendance of people not involved in every item may be able to be restricted so that they 'visit' the meeting when required. Obviously this may be difficult to monitor, particularly if, having given their report and left the meeting, a further matter arises affecting their area of responsibility. However, this is a situation where the Chairman needs to coach members to prepare for reports from such 'visiting executives' and to try to deal with all matters affecting them during their fleeting 'report only' visits.

3. Quorum

Composition guidelines seek to restrict access to the meeting whereas quorum guidelines exist to ensure that at least a minimum number of entitled persons are present (see QUORUM for more details).

4. Apologies

Most meetings will expect members to be present – directors of limited liability companies have a legal obligation to be present at all Board Meetings. Inevitably there will be instances where it is impossible for a person to be present – for example, due to business, holiday or sickness – and where the reason is acceptable. In such instances the member should apologise for their non-attendance and the matter should be recorded in the MINUTES. Some organisation's meetings require their members to sign an attendance book which then provides independent evidence of who was present although this might usefully be recorded in the minutes. The late arrival and early departure of members should also be recorded in the minutes.

Where a member has regular difficulty (for acceptable reasons) in attending meetings either their appointment should be reconsidered or the possibility of them appointing someone to attend in their place should be investigated. Limited liability companies often include in their Articles of Association power for directors to appoint 'alternates' to act in their absence.

5. Punctuality

Late arrival can delay the start of the meeting and wastes the time of those who attended on time. Whilst occasional delays can be understood, the Chairman may need to remind all members that prompt attendance is expected.

6. Resolving the business

The decisions of meetings are taken by passing resolutions. Although this may be true in theory, in practice most Board Meetings' MINUTES will record 'it was agreed that...' meaning that the decision was taken by consensus agreement rather than by means of formal ratification of a resolution. However, it is necessary to maintain a degree of formality in GENERAL MEETINGS where it is important to demonstrate that shareholders have exercised the power given them by their shareholding. There are several types of resolutions.

Checklist

1. Ordinary resolutions
   Every resolution other than that designated Special or Extraordinary (see below) is an ordinary resolution, which can be passed by a simple majority of those shareholders present at the meeting agreeing with the proposal. All shareholders must have been given proper notice of the meeting (unless unanimously they had first agreed to waive notice) but the majority required is only of those who are present in person or by proxy.

   Some ordinary resolutions must be filed with the Registrar of companies. These include those that:
   a) increase the authorised share capital;
   b) authorise the directors to allot shares;
   c) authorise a voluntary winding up of the company; and
   d) revoke an elective resolution (see below).

2. Special resolutions
   Special resolutions require a higher degree of approval by the members. Whereas ordinary resolutions require a bare majority, special resolutions require agreement of 75 per cent of those present in person or by proxy. Twenty-one days' notice must be

given of such resolutions and they must be filed with the Registrar of Companies. Such resolutions are required to:

- alter the objects clause of the memorandum;
- alter the Articles;
- change the name of the company;
- re-register a private company as a public company, an unlimited company as a limited company, or a public company as a private company;
- disapply pre-emption rights of shareholders;
- reduce the company's share capital (which also needs the Court's approval);
- authorise the purchase of the company's own shares or provide assistance to allow purchase of its own shares.

3. Extraordinary resolutions

As indicated by their name such resolutions tend not to be used very often not least since most relate to business arising from winding up. They require 14 days' notice and, like Special Resolutions, can only be passed if 75 per cent of those present in person or by proxy do agree.

Special and extraordinary resolutions can be passed at the Annual General Meeting (and thus would need 21 days' notice since the meeting itself requires that amount of notice) or at an Extraordinary General Meeting which needs 14 days' notice (although if a special resolution is to be considered the meeting will require 21 days' notice since the resolution requires 21 days' notice).

Extraordinary resolutions (a copy of which must be sent to the Registrar) are required for:

- any matter stated by the company's Articles to require an Extraordinary resolution (unless Company Law now requires it to be subject to the requirements of a Special resolution);
- that a company cannot continue in business by reason of its liabilities and should be wound up;
- to grant certain powers to the liquidator in a members' voluntary winding up;
- that assets of the company in a winding up can be distributed to the members in specie.

4. Special notice

As well as the above three types of resolutions (which are expected to be reduced to two under the new Companies Act), the Board must give special notice (i.e. full details) of:

- any resolution relating to an auditor other than for the

re-election of an auditor elected at the previous AGM or to settle his remuneration;
- the removal of a director; or
- (for PLCs and subsidiaries of PLCs only) the appointment or re-election as a director of such a company of a director aged 70 or over.

5. Written resolutions

Providing all shareholders (i.e. there is complete unanimity) agree then any resolution can be passed by a written resolution signed by each shareholder individually and returned to the company (i.e. without the need for them to meet or for a meeting to be convened). All 100 per cent must be in agreement and a note of the resolution must be placed in the Minute Book of shareholder meetings. Note that there are special requirements (mainly relating to the need to give full details) if the subject matter of the resolution is:
- the disapplication of pre-emption rights;
- financial assistance for the purchase of the company's own shares;
- purchase of the company's own shares;
- payment out of capital; and
- approval of director's service contracts.

6. Elective resolutions

With 21 days' notice, Private Limited Companies can pass a number (currently five) 'elective resolutions'. These comprise:
- giving or renewing director's five-year authority to allot shares;
- dispensing with the laying of accounts before a meeting (in this case the accounts must be sent to each member with the proposed elective resolution);
- dispensing with holding of the AGM;
- reducing the percentage required for sanctioning short notice of an Extraordinary General meeting from 95 per cent to 90 per cent; and
- dispensing with the annual re-appointment of Auditors.

All elective resolutions must be filed with the Registrar (within 15 days) as must any resolution (ordinary) revoking them. Should a private company reregister as a public company all elective resolutions are automatically void from the date of reregistration.

Notes

There is nothing to stop an elective resolution being passed using the written resolution procedure [i.e. being passed without a meeting being held].

The Registrar has noted that some companies have tried to file 'written special resolutions' – i.e. a special resolution passed using the written resolution relaxation. There is nothing to stop a special resolution being passed by the written resolution process except that in that case the agreement of all the shareholders rather than 75 per cent of those present at a meeting is required.

---

7. Voting

Experience indicates that most business at most meetings including Board Meetings, is agreed by consensus. Given that, to be effective, the Board must act as a team and despite sometimes divergent views share a common aim, this may not be surprising. However, there may be occasions when consensus is not possible and a formal vote needs to be taken. The voting power of individual members needs to be checked against the terms of reference/appointment, for example:

a) the Chairman may be granted a second or casting vote in the event of an equality of votes;

b) in some instances the Chairman only has a vote where there is an equality of votes;

c) a director with a personal interest in the subject under discussion may not have a vote (and may or may not be able to join in the discussion);

d) where a director(s) is/are 'nominee(s)', for example of a major corporate shareholder (or of the 'senior' partner in a joint venture company), they may have enhanced voting rights in particular circumstances;

and so on.

Once again the Articles need to be referred to, to ensure votes are properly exercised.

The personal role

The résumé of administration referred to above demonstrates the importance of the role of the Secretary. But the role is much more than a simple meeting administrator – particularly in a company where the person holding the position has legal responsibilities. Whilst not a member of a meeting (unless holding a dual appointment) the Secretary must be able to provide a service – particularly one of advising on legal compliance and obligations – to all members of the Board, and particularly the Chairman, of whom the Secretary will often be a confidant and of ensuring that the decisions of the Board are communicated to those affected and implemented. Many companies regard the Secretary as the chief administrative officer of the company and the keeper of the company's conscience. As a result of recommendations of the various committees on corporate governance, the position of the Secretary has been given a more prominent role (a trend likely to be continued in forthcoming company legislation. Thus the Cadbury Committee recommends that all company directors should have access to the Secretary and that should there be any question of the removal of the Secretary, the whole board must discuss the proposal.

Television

Introduction

The rapid development of technology has led to the adoption of what a short time ago would have been considered revolutionary means to inform and communicate particularly, although not exclusively, internally. Although television has been available for 50 years it is only in the last decade that it has been used to provide instant information to those remote from the chief location in an organisation. Increasingly however the use of television will become more widespread. Obviously similar considerations to those explored in VIRTUAL MEETINGS apply although hitherto TV has been used mainly for information provision and only a few organisations have in recent years moved to developing an interactive capability – thus achieving true communication rather than simply providing information.

Subject material

The range of material that is provided is quite extensive (as can be seen from the two case studies below), however previous video programmes have tended to concentrate on financial results and business initiatives. Experience indicates that although it may be difficult to engender complete attention to financial results initially, well-presented information will always gain its adherents (virtually regardless of format), whilst repetition of the information preferably in a similar format will engender increasing attention provided the information itself has credibility (that is, that bad news or aspects of the results are not subjected to censorship of some kind). In many ways the important words in the preceding sentence are 'similar format'. Numeracy levels in the UK are even lower than the poor levels for literacy and thus it is not surprising to learn that many people are repelled by financial and allied data and there may be an instinctive shying away from any document containing such information, no matter how well presented. Familiarity can be a considerable force in gaining the acceptance of the majority. Thus, in developing a programme of employee information, it is important that similar formats are used for successive documentation. The second, third and subsequent reports may then gain greater acceptance simply because they are recognised as documents which have been seen before. Conversely changing documentation format may hinder such acceptance.

Having gained acceptance, ultimately most workforces will come to expect to be provided with such information – the initiation of the process has thus raised expectations. Indeed, very often where the information is well presented and the follow-up briefings are open frank and honest, the initiative can create a considered demand for more information. Subsequently ceasing the programme means that such curiosity now awakened is to be denied, which in turn can destroy the trust of the workforce. This may also create a climate of suspicion as to the reason the information is no longer made available – many people may come to suspect that there is something management wish to hide, and since most people are far more prepared to believe the worst rather than the best that things are seriously wrong. Neither reactions are conducive to good morale – or ultimately to productivity.

The familiarity of the average workforce with television as well as the novelty of seeing an item normally associated with their home in the workplace, may give this format a decided advantage over traditional means of imparting information. However, this must be tempered with the realisation that research into comparisons between retention of information provided in written and video formats disclosed that video achieved a lower result on detail although it was better at conveying themes and overall 'messages'. Similar results may be experienced with TV programmes which should be backed up by with written material for later reading and reference.

Case study:	*Using a modern medium*
	1. Vehicle manufacturer BMW uses TV to inform their staff in over 140 dealerships of the latest information regarding sales, marketing and competitor information. Their programmes are developed on a weekly basis and edited overnight and thus retain the essential immediacy of the news. Initially despite considerable interest, the company found that the one-way flow was restrictive and soon set up a phone link so that staff could phone during short live sessions and ask question of executives 'on screen'.
	2. Problem: How do you contact 37,000 employees at 1,700 units of the largest building society in the

world, when they are spread throughout the
country, so that they receive the same message
virtually simultaneously and can also be
encouraged to respond and interact with those
conveying the news?

Answer: according to the Halifax, set up and use
your own in-house television service. The service,
which added a dimension to the existing, regular,
paper-based employee communication data, cost
£5 million, most of this being the cost of the
installation of satellite receivers and television
and video equipment at all the Society's outlets.

A team of ten, headed by Business TV Controller,
Martin Batt, produce around 60 programmes
each year including a fortnightly business news
service, aimed at all employees plus a monthly
programme which is specifically for sales and
marketing staff.

Although each script is produced by a team of
five in-house writers, the programmes use
professional presenters, who not only report news
but also interview managers on a range of
subjects. The response to the new service has
been enthusiastic, with most employees ranking
Halifax TV equal in value to a face-to-face
briefing with their immediate manager (ranked in
MORI's research to be many employees' most
preferred means of communication) whilst tested
receptivity is extremely high (85–90 per cent) in
the branches.

The service proved of considerable value after the
Halifax merger with Leeds Permanent Building
Society since key issues could be explored and
opportunities and challenges explained.

Traditionally, TV allows information to be
disseminated from source to audience only, but
Halifax has experimented with phones which
allow members of the audience to pose questions
to the presenters and interviewees. 'The problem

there' comments Martin Batt, 'is that you need a long programme to allow time for the audience to assimilate what is being said, and then to consider and pose questions. We have also trialled interactive key pads which enable questions to be posed directly to the presenter by the audience in the branch network.'

Care is taken to brief managers first concerning big news stories (branch reorganisations, changes to terms and conditions, etc.) so that the line of command is preserved. Other than that the local staff watch the programmes as a team – a situation which also allows managers to deal with local matters at the same time.

Regular checking is conducted to test staff reactions. After each programme a sample of 40–50 employees are contacted to gain their reaction and in addition four times each year a sample of 500 employees are tested on their receptivity. So far the response has been extremely good and there is no doubt that the programmes are fulfilling a clear communication need.

Problems? Martin Batt comments: 'It can be easy to be dazzled by the technology, which can have a negative effect. It is, after all, the message which is important rather than the means of conveying the message. A poorly delivered message on TV can be damaging – in some cases more damaging than the lack of a message altogether. We therefore put a lot of emphasis on planning and preparation to ensure we get it right – at least most of the time!'

Creating a demand

Halifax are on record as stating: *'the introduction of the TV programme has wrought a considerable culture change in the organisation, people now look forward to the programme and if we discontinued it the staff would miss it.'* Equally the Board should be in the position of 'missing it' since such programmes provide opportunities:

- for explanation of a variety of issues;
- for correction where ill-informed press comment would otherwise go unanswered (and because it is unanswered may be taken by many to be 'truth');
- for virtually instant conveying of information of urgent matters (which could be particularly useful, for example, in a takeover although all messages might need to be cleared by the Takeover Panel in advance);
- to contradict ill-informed internal rumours or stories.

This last opportunity should not be lightly dismissed. In every organisation there is a grapevine. Where there is a comprehensive communication programme, the grapevine may be less developed than it would be in organisations that seize the initiative in this area. In a recent survey 50 per cent of those asked stated that the only way they received information was via the grapevine although 95 per cent of respondents stated that they had no wish to receive information by this route. Organisations that are wary of generating an information process should take heart since the reality is that far from any adverse reaction to the suggestion, they may find they are 'pushing against an open door'. The problem with the grapevine, as many people know, is that although there may be a kernel of truth buried somewhere within the comment, successive narrators may seek to embellish the truth so that, rather like a game of Chinese Whispers, the result is a travesty of the original. Rumours (which tend to be mainly about bad news) are potentially damaging to the success of the organisation since they undermine the validity of all messages, create an atmosphere of mistrust and inculcate responses and attitudes based on false premises.

Virtual meetings

Introduction

Until the invention of the telephone, although discussions and negotiations could be conducted by post (a long and drawn out process in those days), all meetings had to wait until they could be conducted on a face-to-face basis. Since body language and tone of voice is such an important facet of the message being conducted (research indicates these can account for as much as 93 per cent of the message – effective use of the voice 38 per cent and use of the body 55 per cent – words only accounting for 7 per cent) face-to-face meetings were and still are the most effective means of 'meeting'. However technological advances mean that many meetings are held where the parties are not in the same location. This has clear advantages in terms of avoiding travelling and setting up a swift process for reaching decisions – however there are also disadvantages and these need to be guarded against.

Meetings without walls

A meeting held by electronic connection lacks finite boundaries. In psychological terms finite boundaries can have the effect of binding participants together. In using a room for a meeting the walls themselves can act as a latent force, both separating the members from the outside world and creating a private entity with latent pressure to produce, determine or decide. Remote location meetings lose this 'force of the walls' and can also lose the inherent rapport that being seated within the same room should create within the attitude of the members to the detriment of the meeting. Research indicates that people reach the best decisions when they occupy adjacent physical space – using electronic communication blanks off this advantage.

Case study:	*Creating a team*

One of the seminars I run is a two-day public session which includes as part of its programme, a requirement for the delegates to perform a number of tasks – singly, in pairs, in groups and as an entity. Whilst occasionally there may be two delegates from the same organisation, the vast majority of delegates have never seen each other before and work for a range of organisations operating in diverse areas of business.

By the end of the second day they are usually operating virtually as a team. They experience first hand (and see how their colleagues experience first hand) all the challenges both internal to the course and external to it (not entirely adequate rooms, refreshments, even fire evacuations, included). Whilst the same course could be delivered by remote access at a saving in time and costs, since much of the success of the session depends on the interaction of the delegates themselves, it is difficult to see how the hidden benefits could be obtained. The course would lack its high effectiveness.

This is the challenge to be overcome with virtual meetings.

Work requires social intercourse and, although a number of such relationships, which are forced upon the participants, will be antagonistic, most are not. Most people, 94 per cent is the figure quoted in an American study, want to get along with their fellow-workers and are prepared to compromise their best position in order to attain an acceptable solution. In working with and for other people, we grow to understand them and, even though we may not particularly like them, such propinquity builds relationships, which will help progress to be made. In coming together in a meeting it will be easier to reach agreement or a suitable compromise if one knows and understands the other party than if they are a stranger. Language, gestures, body language (even silences) that emanate from a known colleague are all easier to understand and interpret correctly than those that emanate from a stranger. In contemplating needing to work with people in and out of meetings, getting to know them is perhaps the first requirement. It is for this reason that touring sports teams travel and live closely together, that Boards find they perform better when gathered as an entity in a place remote from the one in which they work, and that a wise supervisor or manager tries to encourage members of the work team to participate in joint activities, and so on. These moves work to create a closer relationship amongst the team to build a rapport and promote better understanding. When those who understand each other come together to discuss problems, there is greater understanding of each others' point of view and a greater chance of agreement. The benefit of this social dimension in terms of gaining agreement and cohesion in meetings is virtually unquantifiable, but extremely valuable. Such value must not be overlooked, particularly if we substitute electronic linkage for adjacent positioning.

Telephone, fax and e-mail

Whilst each of these may be capable of being used to gain an indication of likely support (with the telephone having the advantage of each party being more likely to be able to gauge reaction from tone of voice, enthusiasm, etc. of the other) each lacks the conclusive evidence of agreement. Thus having gained agreement in principle via these methods before moving forward to action decisions it might be wise to ensure original signatures evidencing agreement are collected. Generally for other than the most routine meetings, or in an emergency, it is not thought advisable to use such a means to hold meetings.

Audio-visual links

The problem with the use of telephone, etc. is the lack of body language – although there should be some gain over paper contact since at least language tone can be partly appreciated. This loss can be overcome to a large extent by the provision of audio-visual links. If all the participants in a meeting can both see and hear what everyone else can see and hear (including the reactions of all the other parties) then despite them not being in the same place the matter may be capable of being resolved.

Case study:	*Virtual meetings*
	In 1990 in the case of *Byng* v *London Life*, the Court of Appeal held that a shareholders' meeting could be validly constituted even though all the shareholders were not in the same room provided that there were fully functional mutual audio-visual links in all locations.

Inevitably, the use of remote locations is likely to increase for both types of meetings and providing there are the kind of links set out in the above case study this would not seem to pose too many problems. However, it would be prudent to change the terms of reference of the meeting to encompass holding meetings in this manner. As this book was being finished, the Electronic Communications Bill was making parliamentary progress. It provides that (providing they have permission of shareholders) limited liability companies would be able to communicate with their shareholders by fax or electronic address. This would enable documents (e.g. notices of meetings) to be transmitted in this way as well as enabling the shareholder to send proxies by fax or electronic means. In addition shareholders who had previously given their permission, could be contacted electronically and informed that documents that would otherwise be sent to them (e.g. the report and accounts) were available via the company's WEBSITE.

There is no doubt however that audio-visually linked sites will increasingly be used to hold meetings and those involved need to prepare for this eventuality.

Checklist

1. Consider the location for each participating site. This should ideally be a purpose designed room – a crowded office is likely to pose considerable problems of noise, distraction and lack of confidentiality, not only for those linked from that location but also for those at other locations. The room should be made secure to prevent telephone and person interruptions.
2. Neutral colours should be used in all locations so that the surroundings do not distract. A similar standard of decor and furnishing (also using neutral colours) should be used.
3. Choose the camera location with care. This should be close enough so that those in remote locations can clearly see the expression on the face of the speaker. This is relatively easy with one to one meetings but with multi-member meetings where there are several members in several locations, the reaction of all is important and it may be that two cameras are needed – one giving the close up referred to above and the other an overall shot of all participants.
4. If two cameras are not available to give the coverage suggested in 3, one giving an overall shot should be used. Although it may be possible to alter camera shots (e.g. closing in for close-up shots of the speaker, and panning round) this may become so intrusive that it destroys the rapport being sought.
5. The meeting should be convened in the same way as traditional

meetings, i.e. with an AGENDA which could of course be transmitted by fax or e-mail to save time but nevertheless should still provide sufficient advance notice so that the participants have time to consider the matters for discussion/decision.

6. Participants should attempt to ignore the camera and look at the screen showing the other participants. Many people find themselves mesmerised by the unblinking eye of the camera and tend to stare at it in a way that they would not do when face to face with another person.

7. Video screens tend to magnify voices and movements so these should both be more restrained than in a single-location meeting. Similarly, disagreements and criticism seem to be more pointed when transmitted by camera and screen than in reality and thus these also need to be controlled.

8. Participants should be seated in a reasonably relaxed manner and be prepared to try to interact with their opposite numbers despite being remote from them – e.g. nodding when in agreement with a point being made. They should observe the usual meetings rules of not speaking until the other person has finished.

9. The level of formality of approach, seating, clothing, etc. should all be set down in advance and complied with by all participants. Simple (discreet) clothing and unostentatious jewellery should be suggested to minimise distractions.

10. Side-discussions and passing notes between participants should be discouraged as it can create greater feelings of distrust than if the participants were in the same room. Humour should be restricted.

11. With lengthy meetings there should be an agreed time when refreshments (or even a break) are taken.

12. As for 'real' meetings, MINUTES should be prepared and agreed in the usual way.

13. Before being asked to participate in a live meeting, it may be helpful to allow participants to take part in a dummy run.

Warning

 What is envisaged here is a simple two-site meeting. The example above of the training course with twelve delegates and a leader poses considerable difficulties since much of its success revolves around the interplay between the delegates. If they are located in twelve different locations and the leader in another it belies belief that such interplay can be effected – one can hardly be looking at twelve pictures simultaneously.

Networking

As well as the use within organisations to pass and discuss information between two or more users, thus avoiding them needing to meet, systems are being investigated for both smaller and much larger meetings. Thus to try and deal with the interests of 130,000 creditors in over 20 countries throughout the world, Touche Ross, the receivers of the failed Bank of Commerce and Credit International, investigated the concept of holding the meeting via a satellite link. Other companies are considering holding their general meetings via television links with regional centres. At the other end of the scale, it is considered that part of the reason of the rapid growth in homeworking in the UK has been the easy access of private individuals to such systems. Productivity is considerably enhanced and costs reduced. Although the participants are remote, meetings can take place and business be transacted.

The problem with such systems is that they lack one or more of the essential ingredients that are part and parcel of most meetings. Networking links allow for the speedy transmission of information, but communication, since to use the system all messages need to be machine readable, may be slower than would be the case with a telephone conversation or face to face meeting. A television link allows both parties to see what is on-screen but not what is just out of the reach of the camera's lens. Above all, what is missing is the social aspect of the work ethic and this must not be discounted in considering the effectiveness of the 'non-physical' meeting. Man is a gregarious creature and even though he may be able to achieve far greater productivity through working without travelling and at hours that suit his body clock, he will miss the interplay with others inherent in the work situation. Further, some people are only able to function when they are in a situation where they relate personally to others. Whilst some creative people can work best when they are alone, many will claim to be able to garner and foster ideas only by bouncing them off others. This tends to occur in real meetings, but may be absent in electronic meetings. A spokesman for a leading UK clearing bank, commenting on the introduction of home-based networking, stated: *'This is not to suggest that we shall see a number of companies allowing everyone to stay at home ... we are social animals with other colleagues in the workplace.'*

Note

Research conducted by British Telecom Conferencing indicates that senior managers on average attend six meetings a week and spend nearly four hours each working day in them. In addition 40 per cent of managers spend six hours each week travelling to their meetings.

Obviously virtual meetings could release a considerable amount of 'lost' travel time (although many claim to use some such time to study required background material). The National Economic Research Association predicts that by 2007 audio-video meetings could reduce business travel by around 20 per cent and the Royal Bank of Scotland states that using the process saves it around £70,000 a month in travel costs. European companies are reckoned to spend around £100 billion per year on travel and associated costs. There is no research on how much of this travel is required so that managers can attend meetings but it must be a substantial proportion. Whilst there are many disadvantages with virtual meetings the propensity for saving both money, time and simple travel fatigue of the subject managers, seems considerable.

Website meetings

Introduction

The development of the Internet (which originated in the USA when several educational and research institutions decided to link their computers to share access to their research material – a development that was quickly copied by the US military) has been rapid and all-embracing. In little over a decade the Internet has gone from a science fiction dream to a multi-billion pound industry with over 100 million subscribers to the world wide web in approaching 200 countries. The web is seeing its traffic increase at a phenomenal rate and so rapid has been the take up of the system that some commentators are suggesting that unless a business is linked to the Internet within the next few years, they will not be in business within a further twenty years. In addition, the Henley Centre has estimated that there could be 10 million teleworkers in the UK by the year 2010. Inevitably 'meeting remotely' is here to stay and its incidence is likely to grow. The opportunity provided by the availability of meeting remotely must be exploited but the inherent difficulties also need to be addressed.

Creating a web page

In terms of communication to potential callers (and customers) the web offers organisations the chance to inform all the millions of subscribers world wide of a considerable range of information on them, their products, services, etc. It thus provides a relatively cheap means of promoting the entity and its products and, with an interactive site, of actually taking orders and generating custom. However, the question of the laws governing such transactions need to be considered and to restrict potential liability organisations may need to specify and restrict those with whom they are prepared to trade and to endeavour to stipulate that its terms are an integral part of the contract before a contract is actually completed. In addition, it may need to be made clear that the information at a website provides an 'invitation to treat' (rather as shops display goods in their windows at certain prices) rather than a commitment to supply, in order to avoid the difficulties that may arise should the organisation be unable to meet the demand generated.

However, when a customer visits a store to place an order or buy an item they can ask questions concerning performance, capability, etc., and the ability of the assistant or supplier to provide the answers will determine whether this is a successful meeting or not. It would be foolish to assume that a website cannot do what an assistant can – i.e. provide the answer to all the questions the customer may have. In fact, experience suggests that relatively few assistants may be able to provide the equivalent level of knowledge. This should be a simple challenge to the designer of a website but nevertheless unless the answers to all a caller's questions are provided, calling may not be converted into order placing. This requires considerable input from a range of people – that is, a sample which should try to replicate the range of potential customers.

Instant information

Interactive pages apart, in many respects a basic web page despite the impressive technology, resembles the humblest paper memo. In this it lacks everything identified in this book in being required of a meeting. A memo cannot communicate, neither can the web (although interactive pages are beginning to overcome this deficiency). Its value lies in being able to 'talk words, pictures and ideas to the caller' and to provide information, with the advantage that, being held electronically, the number of words used is infinite (an immense advantage over the memo). The danger is that such information needs to be constantly updated and failure to do so can lead the organisation into legal difficulties.

Case study:	*Cyberfine*
	A leading transatlantic airline displayed details of its fares, including special deals and discounts on its website in the USA. Having checked the website for details, a traveller tried to book a seat on the discount basis shown on the web page. Unfortunately the time limit to take advantage of the discount had expired but no one had either inserted a cut off date in the web information or changed the data when the offer duration expired. The company was fined $14,000 for displaying misleading information.

Key technique

Since the difference in price of the discounted and full price ticket was apparently only $19, one would have thought that someone in the company could have recognised the mistake and honoured the traveller's request to have the ticket at the reduced rate.

Such dangers apart, the demand for websites is growing. The report on a recent survey by leading public relations consultants, Manning Selvage and Leed, states that 'over 74 per cent of companies already have a website or are planning one' mainly for PR purposes. The advantage of a website over traditional methods of providing information to the target audience (press, mailing, etc.) is that it can always be up to date. In theory an operator could be retained to update it as every single item changes – minute by minute if necessary. This level of updating is perhaps unnecessary, but daily updating is entirely practical and monthly is probably essential. Similarly, if the value of the web is to be exploited sponsoring organisations need to consider what those meeting remotely will expect from their site. The great majority of sites are provided using English since it is generally agreed that English is rapidly becoming, if not already, the world's lingua frança. However a large proportion of those with access to the web cannot speak English. In Europe, for example, only 15 per cent use English as a first language, and only 28 per cent speak it at all – a daunting challenge for UK organisations who are told Europe should be their number one market. Accordingly it may be advisable to present a website which is available in say three or four additional languages.

Case study: *Putting your business on the www map*

The owner of the relatively small Adlon Hotel in Stockholm set up a website in order to attract business visitors, which the hotel relies on for its trade. The website was set up not only in English and the Scandinavian languages but also in German, French, Italian and Spanish. In less than a year the site (now expanded into 18 languages) was attracting over 3,000 hits a week and although it has generated business interest, the hotel now has a flourishing tourist trade with the response from those speaking the additional languages accounting for 10 per cent of its total turnover (and 47 per cent of the Internet trade).

Computer-aversion

Despite the rising number of Internet devotees there are still a considerable number of customers who have an aversion to dealing with a machine and yearn for a human voice, particularly if they have a non-standard question which the website's standard information cannot resolve. Organisations should therefore be prepared to offer additional 'live' guidance for individuals with such queries. Again if these are likely to be sourced from a non-English speaker it would be advisable to use numbers which can be identified as emanating from a particular country so it can be answered in the language of the callers of that country.

Yearly timetabling

Introduction

Those familiar with regular meetings (for example, BOARD MEETINGS) will know that very often certain business needs to be considered by the meeting at virtually the same time each year. To ensure that items are not overlooked as well as to help focus the attention of the meeting on both the routine and the extraordinary matters that they should be reviewing, it can be helpful to generate a projection of the range of topics that are likely to be brought forward for the meeting's attention throughout the next period. The preparation of such a list should also assist in ensuring that the meeting plans for the future – after all most meeting members (for example directors) will be expected to drive their department, division, organisation or company forward.

The foundation for the agenda

Obviously the preparation of a yearly timetable cannot substitute for the generation of a detailed AGENDA, but it can act as the foundation covering particularly the routine business onto which selection of items can be grafted the 'one-off' or topical matters for attention.

Example

January

Standard items e.g.	(Approval of previous meeting's minutes
	Management accounts
	Cash flow and solvency
	Capital expenditure
	Sales projection
	Latest raw materials prices
	Contracts
	New legal requirements
	Sealing)
Non-standard	Christmas trading figures

February	(Repeat standard items)
	Half-year figures
	Interim dividend
March	(Repeat standard items)
	Bonuses
April	(Repeat standard items)
	Safety report
May	(Repeat standard items)
	Personnel statistics
June	(Repeat standard items)
	Following year's budget/plan
July	(Repeat standard items)
	Updated statements re interests
	Customer complaints record
	Quarterly report
August	(Repeat standard items)
September	(Repeat standard items)
	Year-end accounts
	Convene AGM
	Proposed final dividend
	Implementation of changes
October	(Repeat standard items)
	Five-year year plan
and so on.	

Advance administration

Many meeting members (regardless of the type of meeting) are busy and overstretched. Congested diaries require that dates of meetings be set for some time ahead and that changes are avoided. Many companies operate a rolling 18-month sequence of Board Meetings where dates for the immediate six months ahead are absolutely firm, for the following six months may be subject to some change and for the final six months may be somewhat more flexible. As the immediate six-month schedule nears its end a further six months is added, and so on. The existence of such a timetable and outline yearly strategy does not preclude of course variation or addition of meetings – it is generated as a guide not as a straitjacket, and as a way of underlining the need to plan for the future.

Zigzaggers and other enemies

Introduction

This section should perhaps be more accurately titled 'coping with' the various destructive participants who could be termed enemies of the (effective) meeting. Here we attempt to identify those meeting members whose input is unsatisfactory, a more important point is suggestions on how to deal with them – assuming, of course, that simple removal is not an option.

Zigzaggers

Whilst following a zigzag path may be essential in climbing a mountain it is obviously the least direct route to the top. The biblical Tower of Babel was a ziggurat – a pyramid-shaped mound surmounted by a temple and reached by a path which wound its way around the pyramid. Zigzaggers can create the confusing sounds and results similar to those of the Tower of Babel as they constantly shift direction in response to which ever 'wind of argument' they feel may be the most strong and thus likely to win through.

Case study: *Ineffective delegation*

The newly appointed Divisional Chief Executive was very pleasant but hardly the type to stand up to his boss, the organisation Chairman who chaired the Divisional Board Meeting. A scheme of work proposed with some conviction by the Chief Executive was completely destroyed when the Chairman opposed it and the Chief Executive did a complete zigzag or about-turn and argued against his own suggestion. The result was not only the discrediting of the plan, but also the discrediting of the chief executive.

Excusers

'I didn't know you wanted it now.'

This implies self-criticism, since any responsible member should either know when data are required, or have the sense to ask. The argument can be countered by laying down the time-limits for every item required to be discussed by the meeting and explaining the implications that flow from the non-appearance of such data, that is the inability to make decisions, delay to projects and disruption to progress, and so on. In MINUTES is incorporated a device which sets out the time by which an item is required which can help nail this kind of excuse.

'It's not our department's responsibility.'

In the case of regularly produced data this can hardly be accepted. If there is genuine misunderstanding regarding the provision of data this must be rectified immediately. Basically, throughout the organisation it needs to be made absolutely clear who is responsible for what and when. The same device in MINUTES sets out the initials of the person responsible so that this excuse cannot be used.

'No one authorised me to proceed.'

Again, if true, the authority process needs to be reconsidered, sorted and clarified. This is a far more widely experienced problem than is often realised, with problems of both commission and omission. The authority and responsibility of meeting members and others, should be clarified and delineated so that the situation and this excuse cannot be used in the future.

'I'm so busy I just can't get round to it.'

There is an old saying that if you want something done you should ask a busy person to do it. If this is so, then this type of excuse tends to be used by people who are unable to organise themselves, irrespective of the amount of time at their disposal. Whilst some patience may be necessary, if repeated, their bluff needs to be called by a suggestion that, in that case, there will need to be a reallocation of duties, or ultimately that it may be necessary to remove the member from the meeting's constitution. This may help concentrate the mind wonderfully.

'We've always done it that way.'

If this is used to explain why data have not been submitted in the way required by the meeting, it may be a genuine response but infers either a lack of attention to, or a lack of clarity in, the original request. In this instance, the need is to ensure the requirements of the meeting are set out with utmost clarity. Lack of comprehension of what was required cannot then be used as an excuse.

'I forgot.'

Hopefully, this kind of excuse will rarely be experienced. The immediate counter is to ensure the minutes are clear, incapable of misinterpretation and issued promptly. They must also specify a time to ensure accountability and be distributed with a covering note stressing the need to comply with items requested. The long-term counter to this excuse may again need to be the removal of the member.

Wet blankets

The fact that some meeting members take a few attempts to achieve what is required is a fact of life – at least they are attempting what is difficult to them. A few gifted individuals seem able to achieve what is required at their first attempt. At the other end of what could be called an 'attainment scale' to such achievers or 'perseverers', are wet blankets, those who actually contribute very little but simply highlight all the problems, real and imagined, and apparently rejoice in failure. Their stock phrase tends to be 'I told you that would happen', and because of their essentially negative attitude they may be of little practical help to most meetings. If it is suspected that they are having a demotivating effect on other members and holding back the successful attainment of the aims of the meeting, it may be necessary to replace them. However, dispensing with someone like this should not be automatic, since on occasion their presence may help. For example, should the meeting consist of a number of other very positive and assertive members whose incautious enthusiasm might lead them into areas from which others might hold back, a 'wet blanket' approach might be a useful dampener and allow further questioning of a project than might otherwise be the case.

Procrastinators

Whilst the application of the occasional wet blanket may be beneficial, particularly where it causes over-enthusiastic members to stop and think again, procrastinators have few redeeming features. Their stock in trade is to demand that a decision be deferred for what may seem to be to everyone else no good reason, or their performance is such that every time achievement is required they seem to have reasons for its non-attainment. To ensure that their performance, or lack of it, does not detract from the meeting performance, the Chairman may need to take a close interest in them. This could include:

- setting accountable targets to try to generate action;
- supporting and guiding them to accomplish what is required of them; and
- constantly progress chasing until action becomes instinctive and their procrastination a thing of the past.

If their performance does not improve, even with the Chairman, 'riding herd on them', replacement may be necessary. Indeed the threat of this may actually be used as an additional goad.

Some managements subscribe to the creed that it is better to take the wrong decision quickly than the right decision too late. If that is the choice then the procrastinators are completely in the wrong meeting.

Bullies

Whilst assertiveness is acceptable, aggression, the tactic implicit in the actions of the bully, cannot be. However, if he or she is otherwise an achiever, most meetings may be loath to dispense with their contribution. The approach to the bully could be:

- let them explode;
- summarise their points, ignoring all emotive aspects and concentrating only on valid facts;
- confront them with alternative facts and contentions without responding to the temper or pressure;
- present the alternative in a way that enables them to save face.

If able to use a face-saving device, an informal word of advice about converting aggression into assertiveness may also help avoid a repetition, particularly if the point is made that next time a face-saver may not be available.

Blamers and moaners

These essentially negative players, usually seek to protect their position by sliding away from any accountability and trying to blame others for their own shortcomings in the process. Whilst some opponents seem oblivious or unconcerned at this unsocial behaviour, others can become extremely annoyed. The effect, irrespective of attitude, is that the effectiveness of the meeting is impaired and thus action needs to be taken as follows:

- confront the offenders with any complaints regarding their attitude lodged by their colleagues;
- ensure the facts of the matter are clearly put forward and only facts are collected in return, that is, not allowing further blame and moans to be made unchallenged;
- avoid sympathy and force objective consideration;
- turn the argument on to them by requesting from them, their suggestions for the way forward.

Unless positive reaction can be forced from them, it may be necessary to replace them as members.

Shafters

This description is applied to those who, forsaking any custom and practice, force through a particular piece of business ignoring any effects that it might have on other meeting members. The principle of dealing with the shafter depends on how the original anti-social behaviour was conducted. If there was an AMBUSH or piece of sharp practice, then the manner of dealing is to constantly refer to it in whatever context seems appropriate, plus perhaps a few that do not. The other meeting members will thus not be able to forget the incident and repeated repetition can indicate the strength of feeling about the 'antisocial' behaviour. The last way to react to a shafter may be to 'turn the other cheek' and ignore the action.

Dissent

Most of the types highlighted in this chapter are dissenters in the widest sense of the word. Because they have, in the main, been displayed in negative terms, this does not mean that all dissent must be bad. Some dissent, for example that thrown up by the devil's advocate (see below) can be effective, whilst some is an essential part of achieving a balance of views, and, indeed, a balanced approach to the projects and business. Nevertheless it is essential that dissent is anticipated, planned for and brought out into the open. If antipathy can be addressed outside and in advance of the meeting, this will not only save the meeting's time, but may also enable it to gain from its apparent unanimity and cohesion. It will also gain since the member's public loss of face will be avoided. Many meeting members react with stubbornness if pressure is brought to bear on them in open meeting, particularly if no face-saver is available, although may be prepared to sublimate their views if tackled in private in advance. If antipathy cannot be negated in this way, then it must be exposed and addressed within the meeting so that it can be overcome, rationalised or simply outvoted.

Devil's advocate

> **Example**
>
> In ecclesiastical circles, the status of 'saint' is granted by the process of canonisation, which is begun by means of a very rigorous quasi-legal examination of the proposal. To ensure that this process is carried out with objectivity, one person, known as a devil's advocate, is required to present a comprehensive case against the proposal, putting forward every argument and fact to try to destroy the recommendation, irrespective of their own personal thoughts on the matter.

From this original usage the term has come to be used for the process whereby a supporter's belief, resolve, evidence and recommendations are severely tested by someone, who may in fact support the contention, but acts as a dedicated opponent. Not only should such an action lay bare all facets of the case, but also it tests the strength of enthusiasm of the proposer to the subject matter. After all if the proposer is lukewarm on the idea then it is unlikely, should it encounter problems, that there will be sufficient commitment to overcome these. Conversely, if the proposer is seen to be totally committed to the proposal, then the person playing 'devil's advocate' should be encouraged and reassured. If enthusiasm is present, then it is likely that obstacles will be tackled very positively, whilst the commitment of the meeting will act as an incentive to most people to work hard for success to enhance their reputation. This twin commitment may provide sufficient support to overcome most obstacles.

Combat

In order to combat potential dissent, the chairman, or the project proposers, or sometimes both, may need to enlist support. This may be either active support from those prepared ultimately to vote with them, or at least tacit support from those not prepared to vote against. In the situation where the meeting is likely to be divided, it is essential that such support is not taken for granted, or left to the time of the meeting to determine. Advance canvassing may be essential. After all the unforeseen can always occur; for example, a member whose support was expected is absent or, worse, totally against the concept.

Applying the random distribution theory, in any selection of eight or ten meeting members, three or four are likely to be in favour of an item of business, two or three are likely to lack interest one way or another leaving perhaps two or three who might oppose the matter. This may actually be too gloomy if one accepts the American research that only 6 per cent of people refuse to 'get along' in most situations. Though the source of this research is impeccable, the experienced meeting member might wish to question why it is that representatives of that 6 per cent always seem to congregate in his meetings, since at times dissenters seem far more numerous than this tiny minority would seem to infer.

However, assuming that there may be at least one and more realistically, two or three opposers to an item of business, the Chairman should ensure that their strength is dissipated. Obviously, seeking them out in advance and endeavouring to neutralise one or more or to do a deal to gain tacit support may well be possible. But if this is not possible and the level of opposition remains, other steps can be taken. For example, it would be a mistake to let them sit together at the meeting as they could appear as a sizeable bloc as well as an effective block on business (see CHAIRING MEETINGS).

Bigmouths

The principle of a bigmouth's operation is to shout very loud and long to enhance reputation but to avoid actually doing anything. Such people can usually talk very convincingly and knowledgeably, making a cogent case and arguing forcefully against any adverse comments, but when it comes to obtaining action however, they slide away from the commitment, often claiming to be so committed already that they cannot contribute to the implementation of the project regarding which they have just been so enthusiastic. Rather like the bully, their presence, if they generate good ideas, may be tolerated, despite the lack of implementation preparedness. However the reaction of their colleagues should be tested, since if they feel aggrieved that they are left to implement ideas put forward by the bigmouth, then the chairman may need to put the latter's commitment on the line. This will entail asking them to implement their own ideas. Should such a commitment be lacking, a declaration, that, in that case, the project should not proceed, may be the ultimate test, the bigmouth being told that it's 'put up or shut up' time.

Meetings, however, do tend to draw unequal contributions from their members. Unless care is taken, and members' contributions are regularly assessed, it is possible for some members to 'hide amongst the trees' and for their lack of contribution to be compensated for by that of others. This is usually acceptable to other members if the 'quiet member' is also an action contributor, that is he or she actually performs outside the meeting in order to help the meeting meet its aims. Conversely irritation and considerable demotivation, can be caused by non-performing 'bigmouths'.

Case study: *Caught*

Ted, a committee member, was becoming irritated by Bill, another member, as, although Bill seemed able to catch the Chairman's eye when comments were invited and to hold the floor and have a great deal to say about most subjects, it was clear to him, though not it seemed to others that in terms of actually doing anything, Bill was always able to slide away and evade responsibility. He sounded out Sue, another member, and found that she agreed.

At the next meeting when Bill commented on a particular item of business, Ted, agreed that his comments were apposite and that he should be asked to carry out the idea. Bill demurred, pleading lack of time.

This was repeated twice in the same meeting, each time Bill having to state publicly that he could not undertake the work. At the end of the meeting, Sue asked the Secretary if he could check through who was doing what. Ted interrupted this run through to comment 'surely that was Bill's idea and he was doing it wasn't he?' Bill was forced to repeat that he wasn't.

At the end of the following meeting when the same tactics were repeated, Ted idly asked Bill if he did not mind that all his suggestions were being followed up by others. This neatly brought the matter to the attention of the Chairman who, having been made aware both of the situation and of the attitude of others on the committee suggested to Bill that either he become accountable or he leave the committee.

Buzzers

A derivative of the 'bigmouth' is the 'buzzer' who like his mentor talks volubly and knowledgeably. However the 'buzzer' lards his talk with buzzwords and phrases which sound very authoritative and learned and yet, if challenged or examined, can be seen to be trite and shallow. The aim of the buzzer is to create an impression of being completely *au fait* with the subject matter even though this may not be the case. The phrase implies the speaker knows exactly what he is talking about and that it is entirely relevant to the discussion, whereas often neither may be true.

Case study:	*Drawing the buzzer's sting*
	The discussion at the meeting concerned the choice of music to be included in the end of term concert. The suggestions included works of Handel and Mozart. After some heated discussion, one member attempted to close off the conversation and dismiss the inclusion of the two items with the phrase 'of course these works by Handel and Mozart are inadequate intellectually'. This fine sounding phrase stopped all discussion, as other members hesitantly agreed. The inclusion of the works was dropped until some time later when another member, having had time to consider the phrase, pointed out that what was wanted was a balanced musical programme and no-one had even claimed the works were adequate intellectually and neither was it relevant. Indeed neither Handel nor Mozart intended them in this way as they wrote to entertain as wide an audience as possible.

Process of communication
– Claude. E. Shennon.
(f)